Excel 2016 Level 1
Student Edition

30 Bird Media
510 Clinton Square
Rochester NY 14604
www.30Bird.com

Excel 2016 Level 1

Student Edition

CEO, 30 Bird Media: Adam A. Wilcox

Series designed by: Clifford J. Coryea, Donald P. Tremblay, and Adam A Wilcox

Managing Editor: Donald P. Tremblay

Instructional Design Lead: Clifford J. Coryea

Copyeditor: Robert S. Kulik

Keytester: Kurt J. Specht

COPYRIGHT © 2016 30 Bird Media LLC. All rights reserved

No part of this work may be reproduced or used in any other form without the prior written consent of the publisher.

Visit www.30bird.com for more information.

Trademarks

Some of the product names and company names used in this book have been used for identification purposes only and may be trademarks or registered trademarks of their respective manufacturers and sellers.

Disclaimer

We reserve the right to revise this publication without notice.

EXEL2016-L1-R10-SCB

Table of Contents

Introduction 1
   Course setup 2

Chapter 1: Fundamentals 3
   Module A: Getting around 4
   Module B: Workbook basics 8

Chapter 2: Creating worksheets 21
   Module A: Entering data 22
   Module B: Formulas 28
   Module C: Functions 35
   Module D: Moving and copying data 43
   Module E: Reference types 50

Chapter 3: Formatting 59
   Module A: Text formatting 60
   Module B: Number formatting 63
   Module C: Alignment 69
   Module D: Borders and highlighting 75
   Module E: Styles and themes 79

Chapter 4: Manipulating data 89
   Module A: Data entry shortcuts 90
   Module B: Paste options 97
   Module C: Inserting, deleting, and hiding 104

Chapter 5: Charts 111
   Module A: Creating charts 112
   Module B: Chart types and elements 117

Chapter 6: Output 127
   Module A: Managing worksheet windows 128
   Module B: Printing worksheets 135
   Module C: Sharing workbooks 146

Chapter 7: Settings and templates 153
   Module A: Workbook options and properties 154
   Module B: Templates 164

Alphabetical Index 171

Introduction

Welcome to *Excel 2016 Level 1*. This course provides the basic concepts and skills to start being productive with Microsoft Excel 2016: How to create, save, share, and print worksheets that contain various kinds of calculations and formatting. This course, and the two that come after it, map to the objectives of the Microsoft Office Core and Expert exams for Excel 2016. Objective coverage is marked throughout the course, and you can download an objective map for the series from http://www.30bird.com.

You will benefit most from this courses if you want to accomplish basic workplace tasks in Excel 2016, or if you want to have a solid foundation for continuing on to become an Excel expert. If you intend to take a Microsoft Office Core or Expert exam for Excel, this course is a good place to start your preparation, but you will need to continue on to other courses in the series to be fully prepared for either exam.

The course assumes you know how to use a computer, and that you're familiar with Microsoft Windows. It does not assume that you've used a different version of Excel or another spreadsheet program before.

After you complete this course, you will know:

- How to open and interact with Excel and how to save and close workbooks
- How to enter various kinds of data, how to enter formulas and functions, how to move and copy data, and how and when to use the various reference types
- How to format text and numbers, how to align text, and how to apply borders and styles to cells and ranges
- About various data-entry shortcuts; how to use paste options; and how to insert, delete, and hide data in your worksheets
- How to create charts, change their type, and insert and control the elements they contain.
- How to split and manage worksheet windows, set print options, print and preview workbooks, create headers and footers, and share workbooks with other users
- About workbook properties, how to check workbooks for accessibility and compatibility issues, and how to use templates

This is the first course in a series. After you complete it, consider going on to the others:

- *Excel 2016: Level 2*
- *Excel 2016: Level 3*

Course setup

To complete this course, each student and instructor needs to have a computer running Excel 2016. Setup instructions and activities are written assuming Windows 10; however, with slight modification the course works using Windows XP Service Pack 3, Windows Vista Service Pack 1, Windows 7, or Windows 8 or 8.1

Hardware requirements for Windows 10 course setup include:

- 1 GHz or faster processor (32- or 64-bit) or SoC
- 1 GB (32-bit) or 2GB (64-bit) RAM
- 25 GB total hard drive space (50GB or more recommended)
- DirectX 9 (or later) video card or integrated graphics, with a minimum of 128 MB of graphics memory
- Monitor with 1280x800 or higher resolution
- Wi-Fi or Ethernet adapter

Software requirements include:

- Windows 10 (or alternative as above)
- Microsoft Excel 2016 or any Microsoft Office 2016 edition that includes Excel
- The Excel 2016 Level 1 data files and PowerPoint slides, available at http://www.30bird.com
- An email application and a working email account for a single exercise in one chapter on attaching a workbook to an email (which can be skipped or demonstrated by the instructor)

Network requirements include:

- An Internet connection in order to complete the exercise on downloading and using a template (which can be skipped or demonstrated by the instructor)

Because the exercises in this course include viewing and changing some Excel defaults, it's recommended to begin with a fresh installation of the software. But this is certainly not necessary. Just be aware that if you are not using a fresh installation, some exercises might work slightly differently and some screens might look slightly different.

1. Install Windows 10, including all recommended updates and service packs. Use a different computer and user name for each student.
2. Install Microsoft Excel 2016 (or Office 2016), using all defaults during installation.
3. Update Excel or Office using Windows Update.
4. Copy the Excel 2016 Level 1 data files to the Documents folder.

Chapter 1: Fundamentals

You will learn:

- How to use the Excel interface to interact with the program, workbooks, and worksheets
- How to open and enter data in a workbook, as well as how to save and close a workbook

Module A: Getting around

The first thing you need to do is start Excel. Once you're in, at the top of the screen you see a set of tools called *the ribbon*. You'll click commands and buttons on the ribbon to get work done.

You will learn:

- How to start Excel
- To identify basic features of a workbook

Starting Excel

In Windows 10, you can start Excel by clicking its tile on the Start menu or its icon on the Task bar.

1. Click **Start** to open the Start menu.
2. There are a couple of ways to start Excel from here:
   - Find and click the Excel 2016 tile.
   - Click **All Apps > Excel 2016**.
     You can also set up icons on the desktop, or anywhere else you like for starting Excel.

The Excel interface

If you've never used Excel, the interface might be intimidating. But if you break it into pieces, it's fairly straightforward.

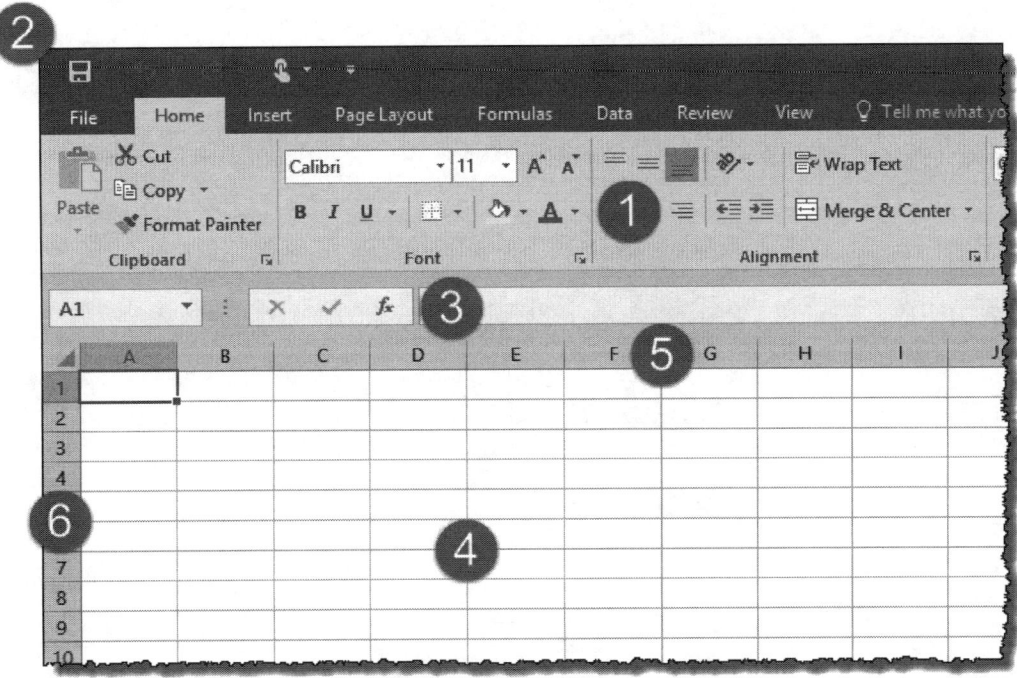

1. *The ribbon* contains groups of buttons, lists, menus, and commands that give you access to the most relevant actions you might want to take. They are *context-sensitive*, meaning that they change depending on where you are and what you're doing. It is organized into tabs (File, Home, and so on), and then within tabs by groups (Clipboard, Font, Alignment, and so on). Get more information about any tool by pointing to it to display a *screen tip* with information about the tool.

2. The *Quick Access toolbar* contains only the most common Excel commands, but you can customize it any way you like.

3. The *formula bar* is where you enter most of the data for your worksheets. It has many features to simplify that process.

4. A *worksheet* is a grid of rows and columns that intersect to form cells. This is where all your information appears.

5. *Column headings* are the letters at the top of the worksheet that identify the columns below.

6. *Row headings* are the numbers to the left of the worksheet that identify the rows to the right.

You enter information in *cells*, which are at the intersections of the rows and columns.

Exercise: Checking out Excel

Before you start, be sure that your computer is on and Windows is running. You'll start Excel and take a look around its interface.

Do This	How & Why
1. Follow your instructor's directions to start Excel.	The method you use depends on your version of Windows and how it is set up. In Windows 10, you can simply click the Excel icon on the taskbar at the bottom of the screen, or click **Start > All Apps** and then click the Excel 2016 tile.
2. Click **Blank workbook**.	To open a new, blank workbook.
3. Observe the Excel window.	Most of the window is taken up by a worksheet, which is just a grid of cells.
4. Observe the column letters and row numbers.	The column letters identify the columns in an Excel workbook. They start at A, go to Z, then start again with AA to AZ, BA to BZ, and so on. There are 16,384 columns in an Excel worksheet, the last one being column XFD. The rows are numbered, and there are well over a million of them. The rows and columns intersect to form cells, which is where you enter and view data.
5. Observe the ribbon.	This is the large area of buttons, lists, menus, and palettes at the top of the window. It's organized into tabs (File, Home, Insert, and so on), and within in a tab, into groups.
6. Observe the Home tab.	It contains the most common commands, and is organized into groups (Clipboard, Font, Alignment, and so on).
7. Point to the **Bold** button.	To display a screen tip, explaining what the tool does.
8. Observe the Quick Access toolbar.	This is the small toolbar at the top left. It has just a few of the most useful commands. You can customize it however you like.
9. Observe the formula bar.	The formula bar is essentially an editing area for the data in a worksheet. Excel has many features to make data entry simple.

Assessment: Getting around

Which of the following are ways to interact with Excel? Choose all that apply.

- Click buttons on the ribbon.
- Use the Start menu.
- Click buttons on the Quick Access toolbar.
- Use the Control Panel.

Excel columns are identified by numbers. True or false?

- True
- False

How many rows are there in an Excel worksheet? Choose the best response.

- About 50,000.
- Under 200,000.
- Over half a million.
- Over a million.

Module B: Workbook basics

Sometimes, you start workbooks from scratch, but more often, you open existing workbooks. Then you make changes and need to save your work. When you're done, you should close the workbook.

You will learn:

- How to open and move through a workbook
- How to enter simple data
- How to save and close a workbook

Opening a workbook

You can open workbooks directly from File Explorer, or from within Excel. Here's how to do it from within Excel:

1. On the ribbon, click the **File** tab.

    The File tab leads to the Backstage view of Excel. Here, you can work with files and set options for the program and for open workbooks. By default, the Open screen appears, giving you the choice of opening a recent workbook, a workbook shared in the cloud on OneDrive, or on your own computer.

2. Click one of the options on the left.

    - Click **This PC** to see a list of the folders within your Documents folder.
    - Click **Browse** to display the Open window.

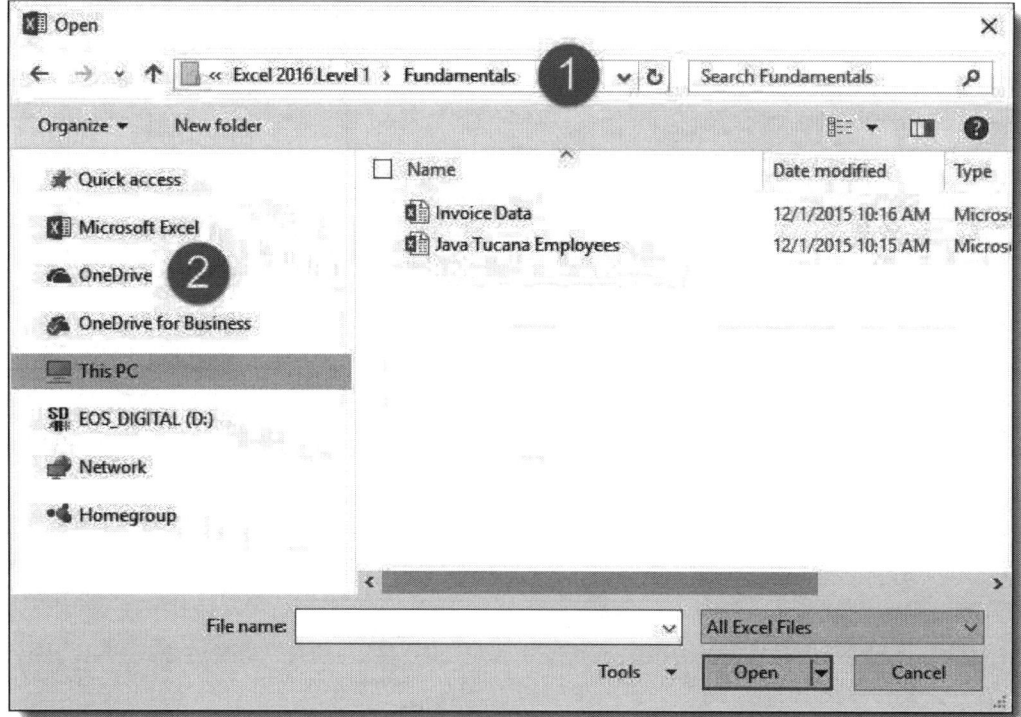

① The *address box* shows your current location in the folder structure.

② The list of places on the left allows you to select devices, folders, and libraries from which to open workbooks or other folders.

3. Navigate to the folder you want by using the address box at the top of the window, the places on the left, and the folders you see.

    You can also search for a file from here.

4. Select the workbook you want to open and click **Open**.

The workbook appears in the Excel window, ready for you to work on it.

Workbook navigation

You can simply click the mouse to move around in a workbook or worksheet. Clicking a cell will make it the *active cell*, meaning that if you type, that's where the information goes. But as worksheets get larger—and they can get very large—you'll need better ways to move around.

 Exam Objective: MOS Excel Core 1.2.2, 1.4.7

Navigation techniques

Technique	What it does
Arrow keys	Move one cell in the direction of the arrow.
Shift+Arrow keys	Move to the last cell that has data in this direction. Or, if the current cell is empty, move to the first cell in this direction that has data. Very useful.
Tab	Move one cell to the right.
Shift+**Tab**	Move one cell to the left.
Home	Move to the first cell in the row.
Ctrl+**Home**	Move to cell A1
Ctrl+**End**	Move to the last cell that contains any data on the worksheet.
Scroll bars	Scroll your view of the worksheet without changing the active cell. You can drag the box to move by a screen, click the arrows to move one row or column at a time, or drag the box to move very quickly. The vertical scroll bar is on the right, the horizontal on the left.
Name box	Enter a cell address (such as "C10") to move to that cell. The name box always displays the active cell.
Zoom	Use the Zoom control on the far right at the bottom of the screen to zoom in or out on the workbook.

Ranges are blocks of cells, and you select them by dragging from one corner of the range to another. You can also select a range by selecting a corner, holding down Shift, and then using arrow keys to extend the selection in any direction.

A workbook can contain many worksheets, arranged in a sort of stack. You can use the worksheet tabs at the bottom of the screen to activate other worksheets. You can also move between workbooks by holding down Ctrl and pressing either Page Up or Page Down.

Chapter 1: Fundamentals

Exercise: Opening and moving through a workbook

Excel is open and the sample data files for this exercise are accessible. In this exercise, you'll open a workbook containing invoice data and reports on that data, and learn to move around using various keyboard and mouse techniques.

Exam Objective: MOS Excel Core 1.2.2, 1.4.7

Do This	How & Why
1. Click the **File** tab.	To display Excel's Backstage view. This is the one ribbon tab that takes you off the ribbon. Backstage view is where you perform actions on files or change settings for workbooks, worksheets, or Excel itself. By default, the Open screen appears, giving you options for opening workbooks. If you've recently opened some workbooks, you'll see them listed here.
2. Click **Browse**.	On the left, under Open in the list of places. Excel's Open window appears.
3. Navigate to the current data folder.	Click **This PC** on the left, then use the list on folders and files on the right. The folder is called "Fundamentals." Your instructor can help you.
4. Select **Invoice Data**, and click **Open**.	
5. Observe the workbook.	It contains invoice data for Java Tucana's sales of boxes of individual servings of coffees and teas for offices. Each row represents one invoice, showing the customer, sales representative, sales region, product, quantity, and amount.
6. Click cell A6.	To select the cell and make it active. This cell contains a label, "Date," that identifies the data in the column below.
7. Observe the Name box.	In the upper left. It shows the *address* of the active cell, which is the column letter followed by the row number.

Do This	How & Why
8. Experiment with the arrow keys.	Pressing an arrow key moves the active cell one row or column in the direction of the arrow.
9. Drag over a range of cells.	To select them. Dragging selects a range, which is a rectangular block of cells. You refer to a range by its upper-left and lower-right corner cells, separated by a colon. For example, A2:C4.
10. Press **Ctrl+Home**.	To make cell A1 active. This can be very handy when you're far from home.
11. Press **Ctrl+End**.	To move to the last cell that contains data, cell H1004. This worksheet has about 1,000 rows of data. That might seem like a lot, but a worksheet can contain far more.
12. Press **Ctrl+Right Arrow**, then **Ctrl+Down Arrow**.	To move to the last cell in the worksheet. A worksheet has over 16,000 columns and over a million rows. That's room for a great deal of data.
13. Experiment with the scroll bars.	The scroll bars allow you to move your view of the worksheet without moving the active cell. The arrows at the top and bottom of the vertical scroll bar move on row up or down, while the arrows to the left and right of the horizontal scroll bar move one column left or right. Dragging the scroll boxes lets you move your view quickly.
14. Experiment with the Zoom control, and then return to 100% magnification.	The zoom control is in the lower-right corner of the Excel window. You drag it to change the level off maginfication in the workbook. — ——I—— + 100%
15. Click the **Reps** worksheet tab.	At the bottom of the screen. To activate the Reps worksheet. This worksheet contains a type of Excel report called a PivotTable which summarizes data by sales rep from the large list of invoices.
16. Activate the Customers worksheet.	Click its worksheet tab. This PivotTable summarizes by Customer.
17. Press **Ctrl+Page Up**.	To move one worksheet up in the stack. The Reps worksheet is now active.
18. Return to cell A1 on the Invoices worksheet.	Activate the worksheet by clicking its tab, then press **Ctrl+Home**.

Finding data

You can find locations and data within workbooks in a number of ways. The Go To command finds different types of data, formatting, and locations within a workbook. Searching lets you locate specific data.

Using Go To

You can use the Go To command to quickly navigate to a particular cell, or to find particular types of data.

 Exam Objective: MOS Excel Core 1.2.2

1. On the Home tab, in the Editing group, click **Find & Select**, then click **Go To**.
2. You can use the Go To window in a few ways.
   - Type a cell reference and click **OK** to go to that cell.
   - Select a reference or region from the list, then click **OK**.
   - Click **Special**, then click a type of data and click **OK** to select all of that kind of data in the active worksheet.

Searching for data

You can use the Find command to search for data such as a name or a particular value.

 Exam Objective: MOS Excel Core 1.2.1

1. On the Home tab, in the Editing group, click **Find & Select**, then click **Find**.
   To display the Find and Replace window. Here, you can enter data for which you want to search.

2. In the Find what box, type the data you want to find.
3. To find the next occurrence of the data, click **Find Next**. To list all found occurrences, click **Find All**.
4. Click **Close**.

Exercise: Finding information in a workbook

The Invoice Data workbook is open, and the Invoices worksheet is active.

   Exam Objective: MOS Excel Core 1.2.1, 1.2.2

Do This	How & Why
1. On the Home tab, in the Editing group, click **Find & Select**.	These commands help you find data and move to certain places in the worksheet.
2. Click **Go To**.	You can also press **F5**. To display the Go To window. You can select a location or enter a reference to a cell you want to select.
3. In the Reference box, type `H1004`, then click **OK**.	To select cell H1004, the last cell in the worksheet that contains data.
4. Find an invoice that is associated with the Rep named "Franklin."	
a) Click **Find & Select**, then click **Find**.	
b) In the Find what box, type `Franklin`.	
c) Click **Find Next**.	To find the first instance of the rep name, "Franklin." Note that the Find & Replace window remains open.
5. Click **Find Next**.	To find another instance of the text, "Franklin," in the worksheet.
6. Click **Close**.	To close the Find & Replace window.

Excel 2016 Level 1

Entering data

Entering and editing data is most of what you do in Excel. There are many kinds of data: numbers, text, dates, and formulas, for example. But the basics of entering data are always the same.

1. Select the cell or range where you want to enter data.
2. Type the data you want to enter.
3. Press **Enter** or click the Enter box (the check mark) on the formula bar.

Exercise: Entering data in a cell

The Invoice Data workbook is open, and the Invoices worksheet is active.

Do This	How & Why
1. Select cell C9.	Lloyd is not the correct sales representative for this invoice, so you will change the data.
2. Type Mc and observe the screen.	Several things happen as Excel goes into editing mode. What you type is beginning to show up in the cell as well as on the formula bar. Excel is also guessing that you want to enter a name that is already in this column, "McCanney."
3. Press **Enter**.	To accept "McCanney" as what you want to enter in the cell.
4. Select cell F9.	This is the Units data for the same invoice. You'll change this number.
5. Type 15 and observe the formula bar.	When you are entering data in a cell, the formula bar gives you options for what to do with what you are entering.
6. Click ✓ .	To enter the new units figure. The Enter button is on the formula bar. You also could have pressed Enter.

Saving workbooks

Any time you change a workbook, you should *save* your changes to some permanent location. You can simply use the save command to use the current name of the workbook and save it to its current location. But if you want to change the name, location, or file type, you need to use the Save As command.

 Note: The first time you save a new workbook, Excel treats the Save command the same as the Save As command, prompting you for a name and location.

Using the Save As command

When you want to change the workbook name, location, or file type, you use the Save As command.

1. Click **File** (on the ribbon).
   To show the Backstage View options. Here, you can get information about the workbook or take action on the file (such as saving, printing, or changing properties).
   Backstage view

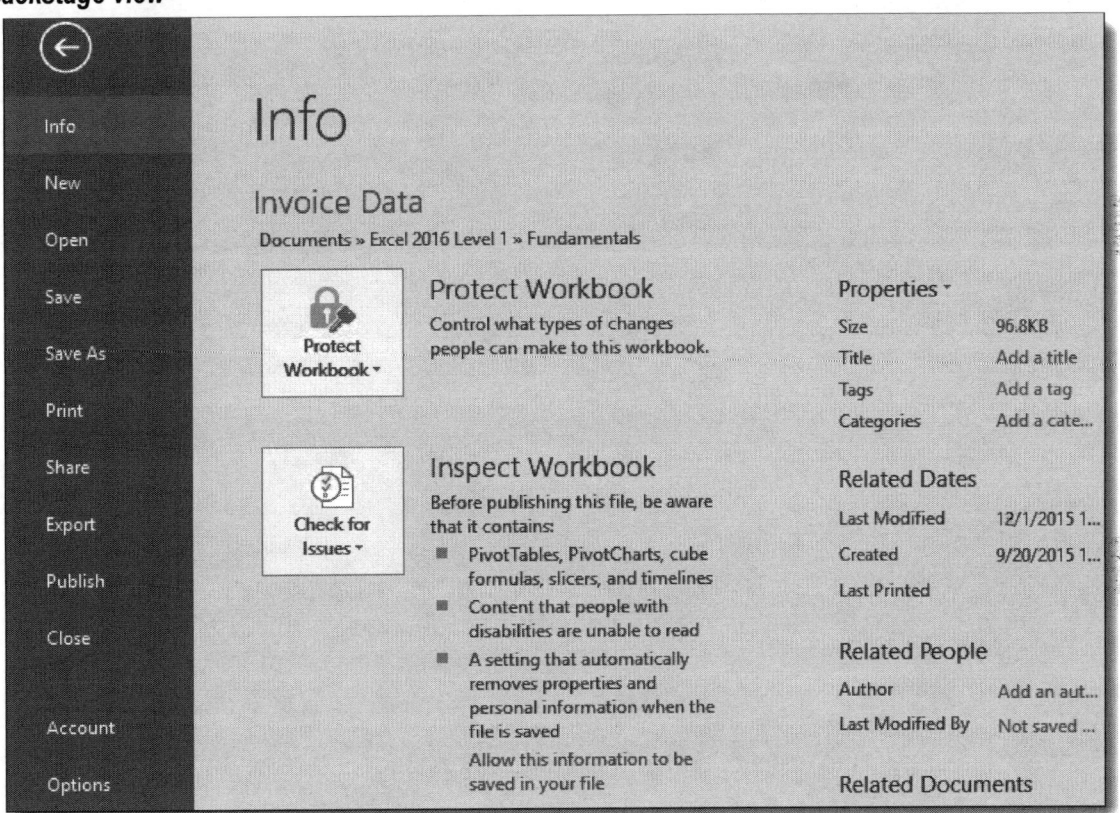

2. Click **Save As**.
   To display options for locations to which you can save the worksheet.

3. If you see the current folder on the right, click it. Otherwise, under Save As, click **Browse**.
   To display the Save As window, which looks and acts just like the Open window. You select a place on the left, then navigate to the folder you want and enter a name for the workbook. You can also change the type of the file (for example, to use it on the web or to share it with people who have an older version of Excel).

   Continued...

The Save As window

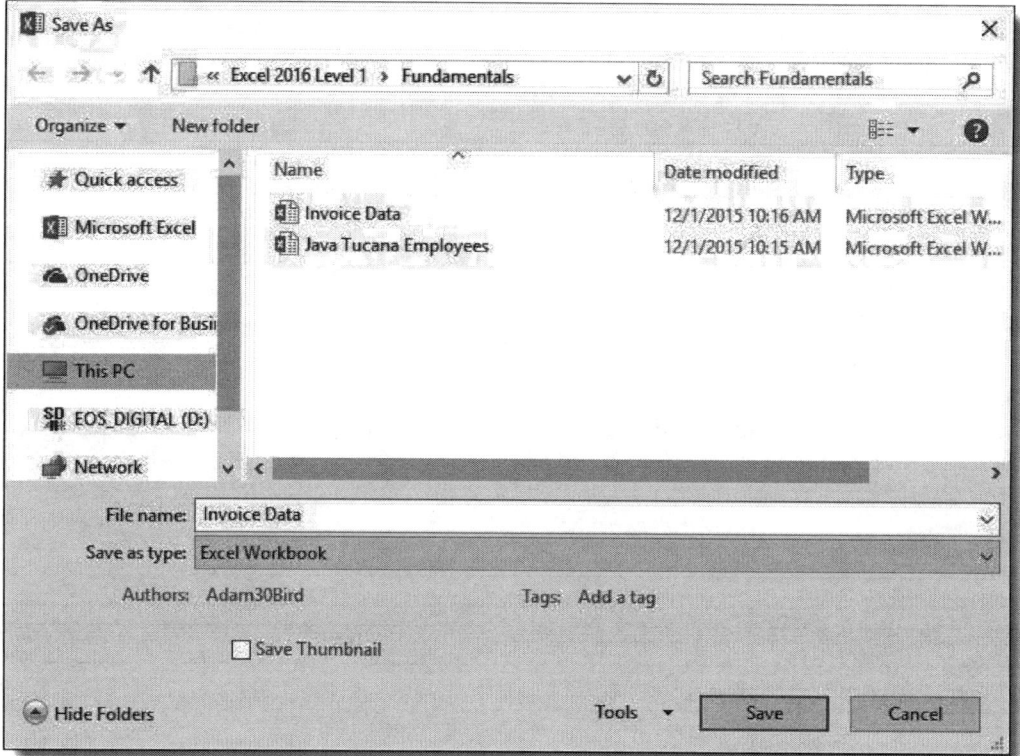

4. Select a location for the workbook.

   Use the places list on the left or the address box at the top of the window.

5. In the File name box, enter a name for the workbook.

6. Click **Save**.

Closing workbooks

When you're done working on a workbook, you should close it. There are a few ways to do that. Whichever method you use, if you've made changes to the workbook since you last saved it, Excel prompts you to save your changes (and you should!).

- Click **File**, then click **Close**.
- Click the **Close** button in the upper right of the workbook window.

To completely exit from Excel 2016, close all the open windows, then click the Close box one more time. You can also do this quickly by right-clicking the Excel icon on the taskbar and then clicking **Close All Windows**.

Exercise: Saving and closing a workbook

The Invoice Data workbook is open, and you've made changes to it in a previous exercise. You'll save the changes you made to the Invoice Data workbook and then close it.

Do This	How & Why
1. Click **File**.	To display Backstage view. This is where you save, print, and perform other actions on workbooks and files.
2. Click **Save As**.	To display locations to which you can save the workbook.
3. On the right, under Current Folder, click **Fundamentals**.	To display the Save As window, with the Fundamentals folder selected. Here, you can change the name, location, or type of file for the workbook. When you open a file, the first save location you wee will always be the currently folder.
4. Change the file name to `My Invoice Data`.	Click in the File Name box, and simply add the word "My" at the beginning. You can edit text in this box as you would anywhere in Windows.
5. Click **Save**.	Note that the title bar now displays the new name of the workbook. `My Invoice Data - Excel`
6. Change the product in cell E9 to `Vela Herbal`.	Select the cell, type "Vela Herbal," and press Enter. Just to make a change in the workbook.
7. Click 💾 .	To save, or update, the file in the current location with the current name. Excel has an automatic saving feature, but it's safest to save periodically so you don't lose any work.
8. Click **File**.	To display Backstage view.
9. Click **Close**.	To close the workbook.

Assessment: Workbook basics

The Open command is on the Edit tab of the ribbon. True or false?

- True
- False

When you use the scroll bars, the active cell does not change. True or false?

- True
- False

Which of the following techniques moves the active cell one column to the right? Choose all that apply.

- Pressing Home.
- Pressing the Right Arrow key.
- Pressing Tab.
- Clicking in the Name box.

Which command do you use if you want to change the name, location, or type of a workbook?

- Save
- Save As

Summary: Fundamentals

You should now know how to:

- Start Excel and identify its main interface elements, including the ribbon, the Quick Access toolbar, and the Formula bar.
- Open a workbook, move around, find data, change data, and save and close a workbook.

Synthesis: Fundamentals

In this chapter synthesis exercise, you'll start Excel, open a workbook of employee data, and change some of that data. Then you'll save your changes and close the workbook.

1. Start Excel (if necessary) and open the Java Tucana Employees workbook (from the `Fundamentals` data folder).
2. Scroll through the workbook to view its data. It contains employee names, departments, and hire dates, and calculates length of service in years.
3. Go to the last cell on the entire worksheet. What is its cell address?
4. Find the last cell that contains data on the worksheet.
5. Find Buford Evangelista and note his years of service.
6. Change Buford Evangelista's hire date to `3/1/2005`. What is his years of service calculation now?
7. Change Rubie Locke's department to `Retail Sales`.
8. Save the workbook as My Java Tucana Employees, in the Fundamentals data folder.
9. Close the workbook.

Chapter 2: Creating worksheets

You will learn:

- How to enter data and about Excel data types
- How to perform calculations using formulas
- About special formulas called functions, and how to use them
- How to move and copy data
- About relative and absolute references, and how and when to use each

Module A: Entering data

In Excel, everything you see in a cell is *data*. There are many types of data in Excel, including numbers, dates, text, logical values, and formulas. You enter data primarily by clicking a cell and typing. But Excel has many tools to make the process simple, and it's important to understand what's going one when you enter various types of data.

You will learn:

- About different Excel data types
- How to enter text and numbers

Types of data

There are actually some subtle distinctions Excel makes behind the scenes involving data types. But most of what you enter in Excel with be either text, numbers of various kinds (quantities, currency amounts, dates, and measurements), or formulas to perform calculations.

Types of data in a worksheet

Expense	Year1	Year2	Year3	Year4	Year5
Rent	24000	24000	24000	25200	25200
Remodeling	12000	2000	2000	2000	2000
Legal	5000	500	500	500	500
Equipment	9000	1000	0	2000	1000
Supplies	12000	13200	0	16000	17600
Advertising	4000	1000	1200	1400	1600
Payroll	60000	65000	80000	90000	100000
Miscellaneous	10000	11000	12000	13000	14000
Totals:	$136,000	$117,700	$135,200	$150,100	$161,900

1 *Text*, which you use to label information. Here, the text identifies what is in the rows (categories of expenses) and the columns (yearly figures).

2 *Numbers*, which can be of various kinds (quantities, currency amounts, dates, and measurements). Here, the numbers represent dollar amounts in the budget.

The other important thing you enter in Excel is formulas. The totals in this figure are calculated using formulas.

Entering text

You enter text the same way you enter any other data, by selecting a cell, typing, and pressing Enter. But Excel handles text in particular ways. By default, text is left-aligned within a cell (though you can, of course, control alignment).

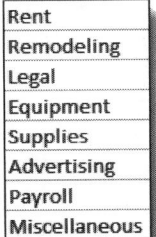

Text that is wider than the column it is in spills over into adjacent cells to the right if there is no data in them, like this:

If there is data in the next cell, then Excel cuts off the text you enter at the border, like this:

Deleting cell contents

You can delete the contents of a cell by selecting it and pressing **Delete**. The same thing works for a range of cells. You can also use the Clear commands in the Editing group on the Home tab, but for simply deleting cell contents, the Delete key is quicker.

Changing column widths

You can widen or narrow a column easily by using the mouse.

 Exam Objective: MOS Excel Core 1.3.7

1. Point to the right border of the column heading for the column you want to change.
   The pointer takes the form of a two-headed arrow, allowing you to drag left or right.

2. Drag the border to change the column width.
   As your drag, a tip appears telling you how wide the column currently is in characters of the standard font.

Creating a new workbook

To start with a blank slate, you'll create a new workbook.

Exam Objective: MOS Excel Core 1.1.1

1. Click **File**, then click **New**.

    To display options for creating a new workbook. You can create a new, blank workbook; use a template; or search online.

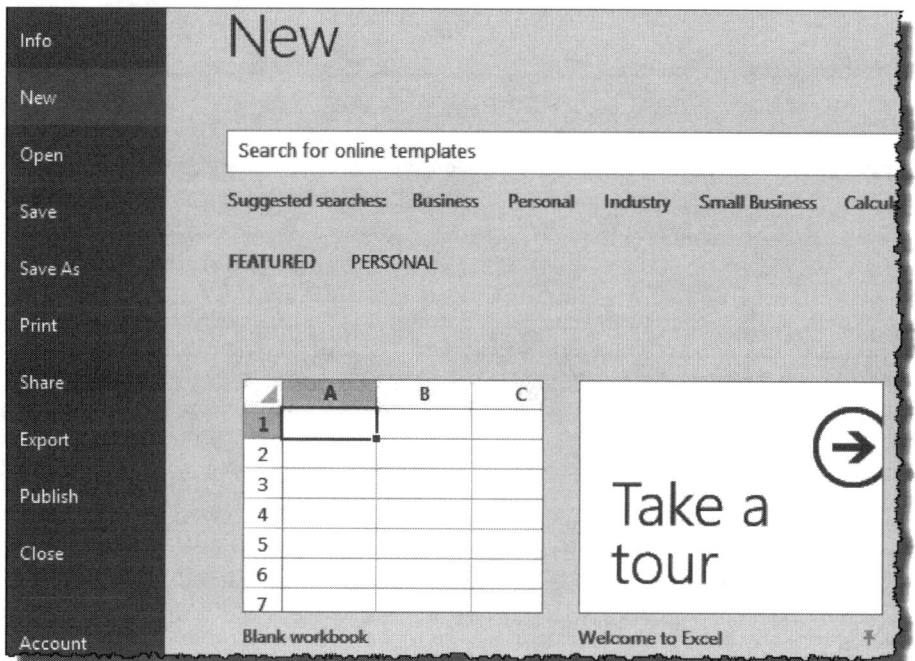

2. Click **Blank workbook**.

A new, blank workbook appears on the screen.

Exercise: Creating a new workbook and entering text

Before you begin, Excel is running on your computer.

Exam Objective: MOS Excel Core 1.1.1, 1.3.7

Do This	How & Why
1. Click **File**, then click **New**.	To display the options for creating a new workbook. You can create a blank workbook, base a new workbook on a template, or search online.
2. Click **Blank workbook**.	A new, blank workbook appears on the screen.
3. Enter `Category` in cell A3.	This label will identify the categories of information below it. Note that when you pressed Enter, the active cell moved down a row to cell A4.
a) Select cell A3.	
b) Type `Category`.	

Do This	How & Why
c) Press **Enter**.	
4. In cell A4, enter `Rent`.	Select cell A4, type "Rent," and press Enter. This is the first category of budget item. Notice that Excel left-aligns text by default. You can control alignment, though.
5. Enter labels in column A as shown.	These labels identify the categories of expenses.

	A	B
3	Category	
4	Rent	
5	Remodeling	
6	Legal	
7	Equipment	
8	Supplies	
9	Advertising	
10	Payroll	
11	Miscellaneous	
12	Totals:	

Do This	How & Why
6. Widen column A.	
a) Observe cell A11.	The text spills into column B. That's fine now, but won't be when you put figures in that column.
b) Point to the border between column headings A and B.	The pointer looks like a two-headed arrow.

	A	B
3	Category	
4	Rent	

Do This	How & Why
c) Drag the border to the right.	To widen the column enough to fit all the labels.
7. Enter labels in row 3 as shown.	These are the year labels for the budget.

	A	B	C
3	Category	Year 1	Year 2
4	Rent		

Do This	How & Why
8. Save the workbook as `My Cafe Budget` in the `Creating Workbooks` folder.	
a) Click **File**, then click **Save**.	
b) Click **Browse**, then navigate to the Creating Worksheets data folder.	Your instructor can help you find it.
c) In the File name box, type `My Cafe Budget`.	
d) Click **Save**.	

Entering numbers

You enter numbers the same way you enter any other data, by selecting a cell and typing. The main difference between text and numbers is that Excel can perform calculations on numbers (you can manipulate text as well, though). If you enter a number that has too many digits to display in a cell, Excel handles that in one of a few ways. You might see number signs rather than a partial number, which would be misleading.

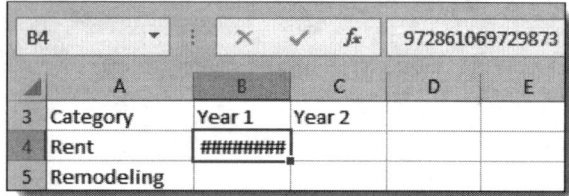

In that case, you can simply widen the cell. If you enter a very large number, Excel might display it in scientific notation:

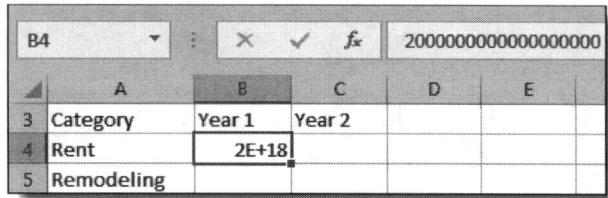

Scientific notation expresses a large number as a small one multiplied by 10 raised to a particular power. Here, Excel represented 2,000,000,000,000,000,000 as 2 times 10^{18}.

If you enter a number with too many decimals to display, Excel rounds off the display, but does not actually round the stored number. Excel also allows you great control over the display of numbers.

By default, Excel right-aligns numbers, which allows them to line up better in a column.

Entering data in a range

You can select a whole range and then quickly enter data in that range.

1. Select the range in which you want to enter the data.
2. Type the data for the first cell, and then press **Enter** or **Tab**.
3. Continue until you've entered all the data you want.

Exercise: Entering numbers in a workbook

The My Cafe Budget workbook is open, and category and year labels have been entered.

Do This	How & Why
1. In cell B4, enter 24000.	Select cell B4, type 24000, and press Enter. To enter a Year 1 rent figure in the budget.
2. Observe cell B4.	The number appears right-aligned in the cell.
3. Select the range B5:B11.	To prepare to enter numbers in the rest of the range. Notice that the range is highlighted, indicated that it is selected. But only the first cell, B5, is active.
4. Type 1200 and press **Enter**.	To enter a Year 1 remodeling budget figure and to move the active cell to B6.

Do This	How & Why
5. Enter the rest of the Year 1 budget figures as shown.	 | | A | B | | 3 | Category | Year 1 | | 4 | Rent | 24000 | | 5 | Remodeling | 1200 | | 6 | Legal | 5000 | | 7 | Equipment | 9000 | | 8 | Supplies | 12000 | | 9 | Advertising | 4000 | | 10 | Payroll | 60000 | | 11 | Miscellaneous | 10000 |
6. Click 💾 .	To save the workbook with its current name in its current location. You could instead press **Ctrl+S**, or click **Save** in Backstage view.
7. Close the workbook.	Click **File**, then click **Close**.

Assessment: Entering data

By default, Excel left-aligns all data that you enter. True or false?

- True
- False

How does Excel handle text that is too wide for the column in which it appears?

- By cutting it off at the right-hand border of the cell.
- By spilling the text over into the next column.
- It depends on what is in the next cell to the right.

You can change the width of a column by using the mouse. True or false?

- True
- False

Which of the following are ways that Excel handles numbers that are too wide for a cell? Choose all that apply.

- Scientific notation
- Binary
- Number signs (####)
- Rounding the stored number

Module B: Formulas

The power of Excel is in *formulas*, which are combinations of numbers, operators, and cell references that perform calculations.

You will learn:

- To identify the elements on an Excel formula
- About worksheet design considerations
- How to perform calculations by entering formulas in cells

About formulas

In order to use formulas to perform calculations, you need to understand their structure.

The elements of a formula

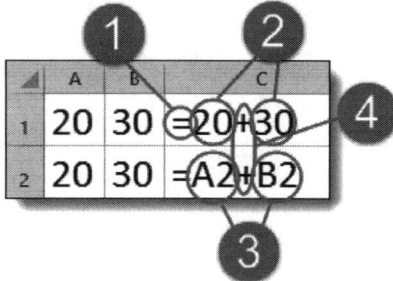

① An *equal sign* (=) tells Excel that what follows will be a formula.

② You can enter *numbers* directly in formulas, but it's not the best approach—if those numbers were to change, you'd need to change the formula as well. In the figure, the first formula adds 20 and 30, but that's all it ever does.

③ *Cell references* make formulas powerful. By referring to a cell, rather than entering a value in the formulas, you make the formula dynamic. That is, if you change a value in a cell to which a formula refers, the formula result updates automatically. In the figure, the second formula adds the values it finds in cells A11 and B11. That result changes whenever those values change.

④ *Operators*, such as the plus sign (+), the minus sign (-), an asterisk for multiplication (*), or a slash for division (/), are the engines by which a formula does its work.

Entering formulas

You always begin to enter a formula by typing the equal sign. Then you enter numbers, cell references, and operators to complete a valid formula.

 Exam Objective: MOS Excel Core 4.1.3

1. Select the cell where you want the formula to appear.
2. Type = (the equal sign).
    The equal sign tells Excel that what follows is a formula. You can create the formula either by editing directly in the cell, or by clicking in the formula bar.
3. Enter numbers, cell references, and operators to create a valid formula.

- Enter cell references either by typing them, or by clicking the cell to which you want to refer. When you enter a valid reference, Excel will highlight the cell or range to which the reference occurs. This is a nice way to visually check whether you're referring to the right thing.
- Enter operators, such as plus signs (+), minus signs (-), asterisks for multiplication (*), or slashes for division (/), by typing them in the proper place in the formula.
- Enter numbers by typing them where you want them in the formula.

4. Press **Enter** or click the enter box on the formula bar to complete the formula.

If you've entered a valid formula, Excel displays the result in the cell. Sometimes, the formula is valid, but the result is an error, such as when you've divided by zero without realizing it. If you make a mistake that makes the formula invalid, Excel displays a message prompting you to fix the problem. You can also enter formulas that while valid, and not resulting in an error, are just wrong. Think carefully about what you want to do before you enter a formula.

Worksheet design

One of the best things about Excel is that you can decide the best way to enter and present your data. It is essentially a blank grid in which you can do almost anything. But people have expectations about how data appears in a grid, and there are some good reasons for those expectations.

In general, you should always put formulas either to the right of the values they act upon or below them. This is what people expect to see, but it also helps you to maintain your workbooks and understand and make changes to them when you return to them after a period of not working with them. This is good:

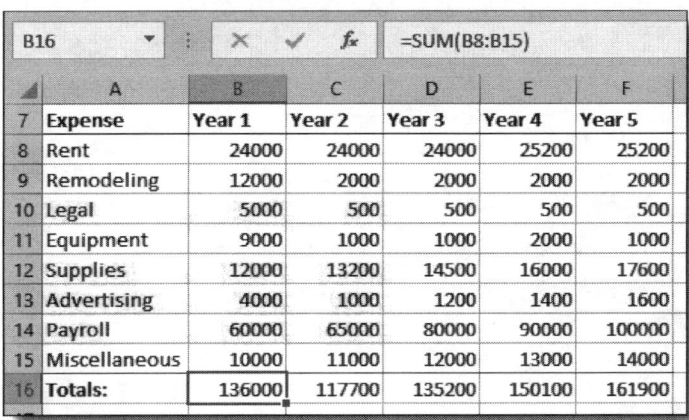

But this would be weird:

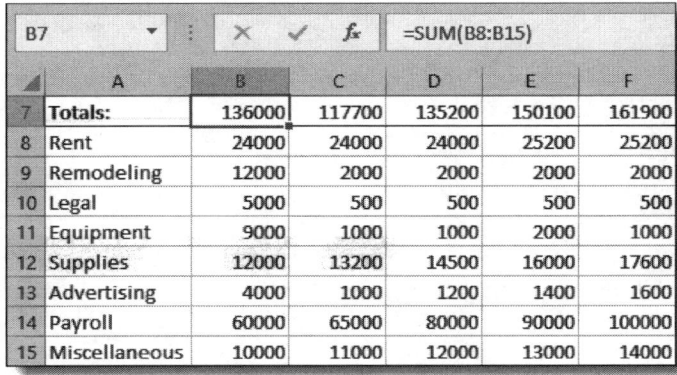

Exercise: Performing calculations with formulas

In this exercise, you'll open the framework of a café budget, and then enter simple formulas to calculate totals and monthly figures.

Exam Objective: MOS Excel Core 4.1.1

Do This	How & Why
1. Open Formula Basics.	It is in the Creating Worksheets data folder. The first worksheet in the workbook has labels and some values for a café budget.
2. Enter a total formula in D8.	
a) Select cell D8.	You'll enter a formula to total the Year 1 and Year 2 rent values.
b) Type =.	To begin to enter a formula. All formulas start with any equal sign.
c) Type B8.	This is the cell reference for the Year 1 rent value. Always use cell references in formulas, if you can. Notice that after you type the reference, Excel highlights the cell.
d) Type +C8.	The formula will add the value cell B8 to the value in cell C8. Excel highlights C8 in a different color. In this way, Excel lets you see all the cells or ranges to which your formula refers.
e) Press **Enter**.	To enter the formula. The cell now displays the correct total, 48000.
3. Select D8.	The cell displays the result, but if you look at the formula bar, you see the formula that you entered.
	 | | A | B | C | D | |---|---|---|---|---| | 7 | Expense | Year1 | Year2 | Total | | 8 | Rent | 24000 | 24000 | 48000 | (D8 formula bar: =B8+C8)
4. How would you calculate the monthly average rent?	You would divide the two-year total by 24, the number of months in two years.
5. In E8, enter the correct formula.	
a) Select E8 and type =.	
b) Click cell D8.	To enter a reference to it in the formula you are creating. You can enter references using the mouse, and it's often much easier to do it that way.
c) Type /24.	

Do This	How & Why
d) Enter the formula.	Either by pressing Enter or clicking the Enter button on the formula bar. The average monthly rent for the first two years is 2000.
6. Enter the total and monthly formulas for remodeling.	The worksheet should look like this when you finish. You could enter the rest of the formulas in the same manner, but you'll be learning better ways.
7. Save the workbook as My Formula Basics.	
8. In C9, enter 4000.	To change the Year 2 remodeling expense figure. Notice that the formulas in cells D9 and E9 display updated values. This is the power of using formulas that operate on cell references.
9. Save the workbook.	Click the Save button.

Order of operations

Excel evaluates the operations in a formula according to its *order of operations*. If you remember a bit of basic algebra, this will be familiar to you. The order is summarized in the following table.

Order of operations

Order	Operation	Operator	Example
1	Parentheses	()	=3*(A2+A3)
2	Negation	-	=-2
3	Percentage	%	=25%
4	Exponents	^	=A4^2
5	Multiplication	*	=A2*A3
5	Division	/	=A2/A3
6	Addition	+	=A2+A3
6	Subtraction	-	=A2-A3

Excel 2016 Level 1

Note that multiplication and division have the same order of precedence, as do addition and subtraction.

Parentheses are the tools you use to control and override the order of operations. If you want to add cells A1 and A2 and then divide that sum by cell A3, this formula won't work:

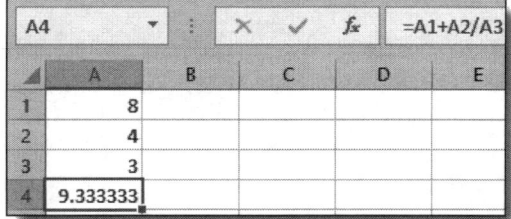

But this one will:

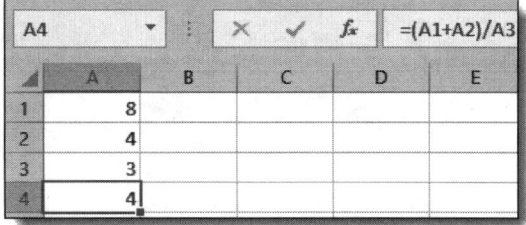

Revising formulas
You revise a formula by editing it, just as you would any text. Here's how:

1. Select the cell containing the formula you want to edit.
2. Edit the formula in one of the following ways.
   - Double-click the cell to edit in the cell.
   - Press **F2** to edit in the cell.
   - Click in the formula bar to edit there.
3. Make your changes and enter the formula.

Exercise: Controlling the order of operations

The My Formula Basics workbook is open. You'll experiment with the order of operations in Excel formulas.

Exam Objective: MOS Excel Core 4.1.2

Do This	How & Why
1. Click the **Order of Operations** worksheet tab.	To activate the worksheet. The worksheet tabs are at the bottom of the window. This worksheet has some very simple sample data for experimenting with the order of operations.
2. Observe A1:D2.	This range contains a cost for an order of boxes, a cost for an order of wrapping paper, and the number of wrapped boxes that resulted from those orders. You'll calculate the average cost per wrapped box.
3. In D2, enter =A2+B2/C2.	To calculate the average cost. This seems like a reasonable formula, but it gets the wrong result, 2.75, because Excel evaluates the division (B2/C2) before the addition. You want to evaluate the addition first.
4. Revise the formula to read =(A2+B2)/C2.	
a) Select D2, and click in the formula bar.	To begin to edit the formula.
b) Insert parentheses as shown.	Click where you want each character, then type it. If you make a mistake, press Esc and start again.
c) Enter the formula.	Now, the calculation is correct (1.25).
5. Observe F1:H2.	Here, you see the costs of two items. In cell H2, you'll enter a formula to calculate the tax, at a rate of 8%, on both items.
6. In H2, enter =8%*F2+G2.	The result, 8.32, is incorrect. Excel first converts 8% to .08, then multiplies it by the value in F2. You need to force Excel to add F2 and G2 first.
7. Revise the formula to read =8%*(F2+G2).	Now the formula shows the correct result, 0.96.
8. Save and close the workbook.	

Assessment: Formulas

Which of the following signals the beginning of a formula?

- Apostrophe (')
- Equal sign (=)
- Any cell reference.
- The letter f.

It is good practice to put formulas in the first column of a worksheet. True or false?

- True.
- False.

Which of the following is evaluated last in the Excel order of operations?

- Multiplication
- Subtraction
- Percentage
- Exponents

Which of the following are ways to edit a formula in Excel? Choose all that apply.

- Double-click a cell.
- Press F2.
- Press Esc.
- Click in the formula bar.

Module C: Functions

Functions are named formulas built into Excel to help you perform all sorts of calculations. For examples, the SUM() function adds up values, and AVERAGE() takes an average. Excel has hundreds of built-in functions, and you can combine them in endless ways.

You will learn:

- About special formulas called functions
- How to enter functions and function arguments to perform calculations

About functions

All functions are formulas, so they all start with an equal sign (=). After that, a function has three main parts.

Structure of a function

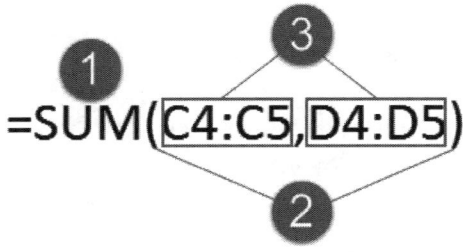

1. The *function name* tells Excel which function to use. If you enter a valid function name, Excel capitalizes it when you enter it. In this example, we have the SUM() function.

2. *Parentheses* enclose the values on which the function acts.

3. *Arguments* are the values, or references to values, on which the function takes action. Arguments can be values or references, but the values to which you refer must be appropriate to the function. For example, it wouldn't make sense to calculate an average of several text labels. You separate arguments in a function with a comma. In this SUM() function, there are two arguments: the ranges C4:C5 and D4:D5. The function calculates the total of the values in both ranges.

Entering functions

Excel provides many tools to help you enter functions. The basic process works like this.

 Exam Objective: MOS Excel Core 4.2.1

1. Select the cell where you want the function.
2. Type = and begin to type the name of the function.

    As you begin to type letters, Excel displays a list of function names from which you can choose. If you're editing on the formula bar, the list appears there rather than next to the cell.

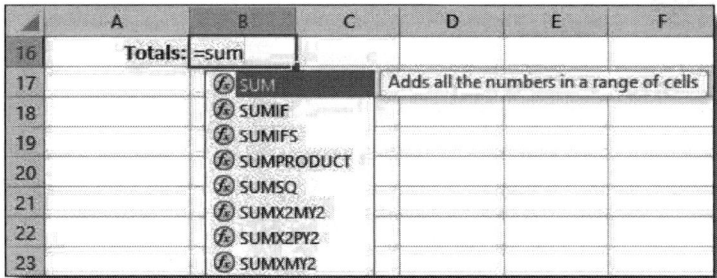

3. Finish typing the name of the function by typing an opening parenthesis, or select the name from the list, and press **Tab**.

    Excel displays a tip box showing you what kinds of arguments the function expects. Required arguments are bold, while optional ones aren't. The SUM() function, for example, requires at least one number argument but can take many more, if you like.

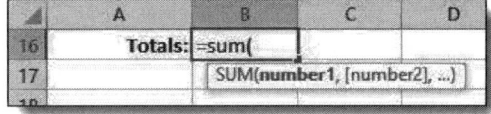

4. Enter the arguments for the function.
    - Type values or cell references.
    - Click cells or drag over ranges to enter references to them.
    - Separate arguments by typing a comma.
5. Type a closing parenthesis, then press **Enter**.

If you've entered a valid function with valid arguments, it will be entered and the result will appear in the cell. If you've entered an invalid function, Excel might prompt you to fix it before you can enter it, or you might see an error value in the cell.

Exercise: Using functions to calculate sums and averages

In this exercise, you'll open a budget workbook and enter functions to calculate totals and averages.

 Exam Objective: MOS Excel Core 4.1.2, 4.1.5

Do This	How & Why
1. Open Budget Functions.	From the Creating Workbooks data folder. This workbook contains the sample cafe budget figures for five years.
2. In B16, enter the correct SUM() function.	

Do This	How & Why
a) Select cell B16 and type =.	To begin to enter the function.
b) Type sum.	As you type, Excel displays a list of functions that begin with the letters "sum." You can simply type the whole function name, or select it from this list.
c) Type (.	The open parenthesis signals that you have completed the function name and will now enter arguments for the function.
d) Type B8:B15.	The function will calculate the total Year1 expenses.
e) Type) and press **Enter**.	To complete the function. The closing parenthesis is the last piece of every function, enclosing the arguments. The cell displays the correct total, 136000.

3. In C16, enter the SUM() function.

a) In C16, type =sum(.	The name of the function and the opening parentheses. You'll enter the argument with the mouse this time.
b) Select C8:C15.	To enter a reference to that range as the argument for the SUM() function. In most cases, this is much easier and more accurate than typing the reference.

Year1	Year2	Year3	Year4
24000	24000	24000	252
12000	2000	2000	2
5000	500	500	5
9000	1000	1000	20
12000	13200	14500	160
4000	1000	1200	14
60000	65000	80000	90
10000	11000	12000	130
136000	=sum(C8:C15		
	SUM(**number1**, [number2], ...)		

c) Type) and press **Enter**.	To complete and enter the function.

4. In G8, enter the correct AVERAGE() function.

a) Select G8, click the formula bar, and type =av.	This time, you'll enter the function on the formula bar. Excel displays a list of functions beginning with "av."
b) In the list, click **AVERAGE**, then press **Tab**.	Notice that when you use this method, Excel inserts the opening parenthesis for you.
c) Enter B8:F8 as the argument.	Either by typing or by using the mouse.
d) Complete and enter the function.	Type the closing parenthesis and press Enter.

5. Save the workbook as My Budget Functions.

Inserting functions

The Insert Function button on the formula bar can guide you through the process of entering functions. It's easier to just type in a simple function, but for more complex functions, with many arguments of many data types, using this feature can be enormously helpful.

1. Select the cell in which you want the function.

2. On the formula bar, click f_x .
   To display the Insert Function window, which takes you through a step-by-step process for entering functions.

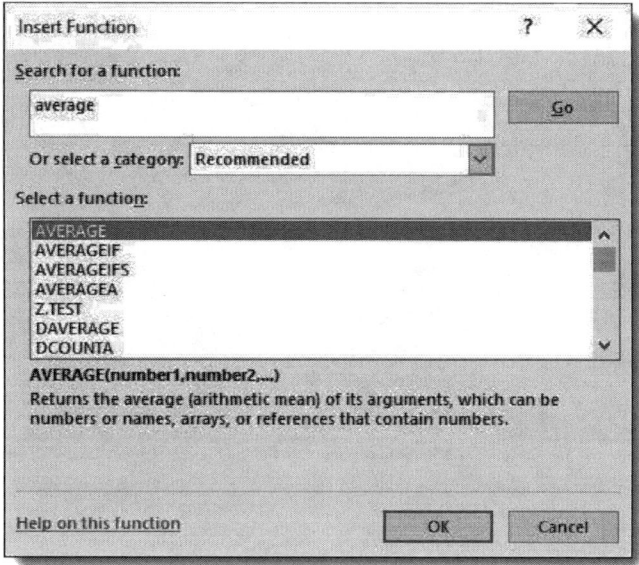

3. Find and select the function you want.
   - Use the "Search for a function" box to find the function you want.
   - Narrow your choices by selecting a category from the "Or select a category" list.
   - Select a function to view a description of it.

4. Click **OK**.
   To open the Function Arguments window. Here, you can type or use the mouse to enter arguments.

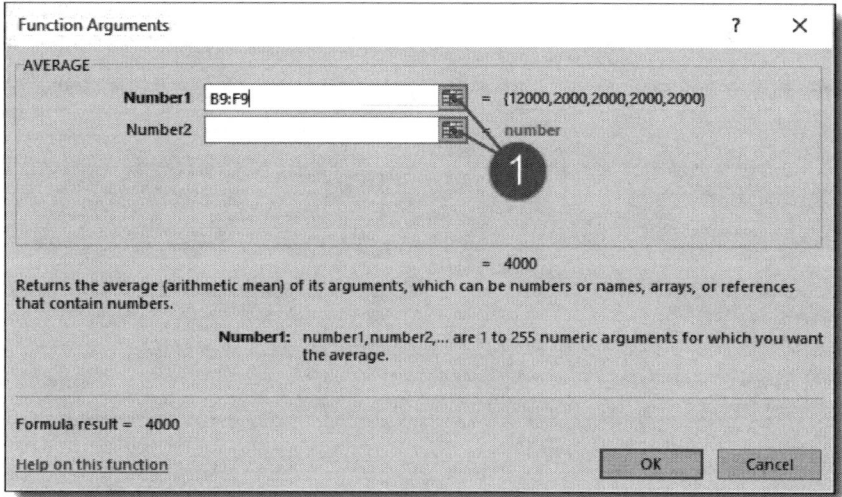

   ① Click the *collapse buttons* to minimize the Function Arguments window so you can more easily select argument ranges.

5. Enter the arguments you want.

    You can type in the argument boxes or use the mouse. If the window is in the way, use the collapse buttons to make it smaller.

6. Click **OK**.

Exercise: Inserting a function

The My Budget Functions workbook is open. You'll calculate an average by using the Insert Function feature.

Do This	How & Why
1. Clear the contents of G8.	Select G8 and press **Delete**. You're going to enter the function in a different way.
2. Select G8, then, on the formula bar, click f_x .	To display the Insert Function window.
3. Search for AVERAGE(). a) In the Search for a function box, type `average`. b) Click **Go**.	 To display a list of functions relating to averages.
4. In the Select a function list, click **AVERAGE**.	The window shows a description of the selected function. Select a function: AVERAGE AVERAGEIF AVERAGEIFS AVERAGEA Z.TEST DAVERAGE DCOUNTA AVERAGE(number1,number2,...) Returns the average (arithmetic mean) of its arguments, which can be numbers or names, arrays, or references that contain numbers.
5. Click **OK**.	To display the Function Arguments window. Here, you can enter arguments in a variety of ways. The window also tells you what kind of argument is expected (number, text, etc.). Notice that Excel has correctly guessed that you want to use the range of values immediately to the left (B8:F8). If it guessed wrong, you can type a reference or use the mouse to enter one. AVERAGE Number1 B8:F8 Number2
6. Click **OK**.	The correct formula is entered and the result, 24480, appears in the cell.
7. Save the workbook.	

Using AutoSum to enter functions

AutoSum is a wonderful time-saving feature that allows you to enter functions like SUM() and AVERAGE() in a single click. You can use AutoSum on a single cell, or to enter a similar function in a range of cells all at once.

1. Select the cell or cells in which you want the function or functions to go.
2. Click the **AutoSum** button to enter the SUM() function, or click the button's drop-down arrow to select a different function.

    The AutoSum button is on the far right of the Home tab, in the Editing group.

    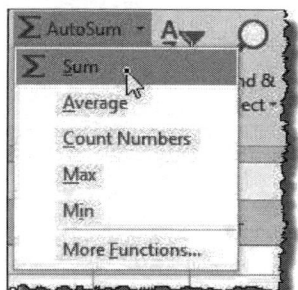

    The function appears in the cell, with a guess at the range you want to use as the argument.
3. If necessary, edit the argument.
4. Press **Enter**.

    If you selected a range of cells, Excel goes ahead and enter all the functions without a separate step for editing the arguments. This gives you less control, but it gets a lot done quickly.

Exercise: Using AutoSum to enter SUM() and AVERAGE()

My Budget Functions is open.

Do This	How & Why
1. Select D16.	
2. On the Home tab, in the Editing group, click **AutoSum**.	The Editing group is on the far right of the ribbon. Excel enters the SUM() function, and guesses, correctly, that you want to use D8:D15 as the argument.
3. Press **Enter**.	
4. Select E16:F16.	Next, you'll enter the remaining SUM() functions in a single step.
5. Click **AutoSum**.	Excel enters the correct function in both cells with a single click.
6. Delete the contents of D8.	Select G8 and press **Delete**. You'll enter the remaining AVERAGE() functions with a single click.
7. Select G8:G16.	

Do This	How & Why
Note: This method works nicely when all of the data are well ordered. Sometimes, however, trying to enter multiple functions in this manner can lead to unexpected results.	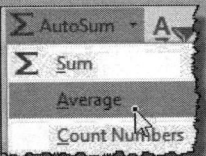
8. Click the drop-down arrow next to the AutoSum button, then click **Average**.	Excel enters the correct AVERAGE() functions in the entire selected range.
9. Save and close the workbook.	

The completed My Budget Functions workbook

	B	C	D	E	F	G
	Year1	Year2	Year3	Year4	Year5	Average
8	24000	24000	24000	25200	25200	24480
9	12000	2000	2000	2000	2000	4000
10	5000	500	500	500	500	1400
11	9000	1000	1000	2000	1000	2800
12	12000	13200	14500	16000	17600	14660
13	4000	1000	1200	1400	1600	1840
14	60000	65000	80000	90000	100000	79000
15	10000	11000	12000	13000	14000	12000
16	136000	117700	135200	150100	161900	140180

G8 =AVERAGE(B8:F8)

Assessment: Functions

Functions are a type of formula. True or False?

- True
- False

Functions can be entered only in the formula bar. True or False?

- True
- False

Which of the following is the name for the values on which a function takes action or performs calculations?

- Variables
- Parameters
- Arguments

Which of the following are ways that you can enter function arguments?

- Typing.
- The mouse.
- The Insert Arguments button.
- The Function Arguments window.

AutoSum can be used to enter only SUM() functions. True or False?

- True
- False

Module D: Moving and copying data

Excel provides many methods for moving and copying data. You can use the Cut and Paste commands to move, or the Copy and Paste commands to copy. All have convenient keyboard shortcuts, and if you prefer the mouse, you can move and copy without commands at all by dragging.

When you move a formula, Excel updates any references they contain relative to the new location of the formula.

You will learn:

- How to move data within a worksheet by cutting and pasting
- How to copy data by copying and pasting
- How to move and copy data by dragging
- How Excel handles a moved or copied formula

Moving data

There are many ways to move data from one location to another. The basic procedure is simple.

 Exam Objective: MOS Excel Core 2.1.2

1. Select the data you want to move.
2. Click the **Cut** button or press **Ctrl+X**.
    It's on the left of the Home tab, in the Clipboard group. You see a *marquee* around the cut data, indicating that Excel has placed the data you cut in a holding spot called *the clipboard*. Excel doesn't remove it from the original location until you actually paste it somewhere.
3. Select the location to which you want to move the cut data.
4. Click the **Paste** button or press **Ctrl+V**.

The data appears in the new location and is removed from the original location. When you paste cut data, you actually have many options about how to paste it. Also, the data remains on the clipboard so you can paste it to multiple locations.

Moving data by dragging

Perhaps the simplest way to move data is by dragging it from one location to another.

1. Select the data you want to move.
2. Point to the border of the selected data.
   The pointer takes the shape of a four-headed arrow.

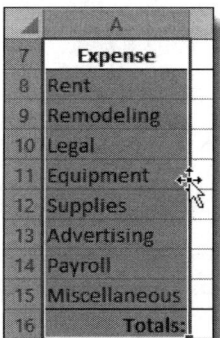

3. Drag the data to a new location, then release the mouse.

The data appear in the new location and is removed from the original location.

Undoing actions

You can undo the last action you performed by clicking the Undo button on the Quick Launch toolbar or by pressing Ctrl+Z.

The Undo and Redo buttons

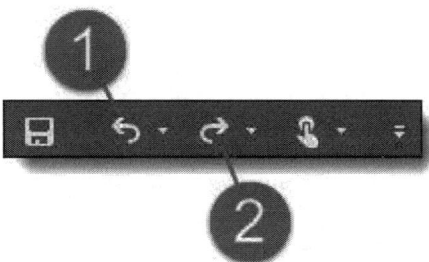

1. The *Undo button* undoes the last action or actions you performed.

2. The *Redo button* repeats the last action or actions you performed.

Exercise: Moving data in a worksheet

In this exercise, you'll open a workbook showing a year of a café budget, and move that data using a couple of techniques.

 Exam Objective: MOS Excel Core 2.1.3

Do This	How & Why
1. Open Moving and Copying.	From the Creating Worksheets data folder. This workbook contains a first-year budget for a café. We'd like to move the budget info down a few rows.
2. Move the budget info down three rows. a) Select A7:N16. b) Click **Cut**.	The Cut button is on the ribbon's Home tab, in the Clipboard group. A marquee appears around the cut data, telling you that you've placed it on the clipboard, ready to move.
c) Select A10. d) Click the **Paste** button.	The Paste button is next to the Cut button. The budget data now begins in row 10.
3. On the Quick Launch toolbar, click .	This is the Undo button. Very useful. You can also press **Ctrl+Z** to undo the last action. The budget moves back where it was.
4. Select A7:N16.	This time, you'll move the data down by dragging it.
5. Move the data down by dragging. a) Point to the border of the selected data.	This pointer shape, a four-headed arrow, tells you that you can drag the data.
b) Drag the data down a few rows.	Simply release the mouse when the data is where you want it. The data appears where you release the mouse.
6. Undo the move.	Click the Undo button or press Ctrl+Z.
7. Save the workbook as `My Moving and Copying`.	

Excel 2016 Level 1

Copying data

Often, you want to create data that is identical to or similar to data you already have. For example, you'll likely use similar labels for similar budgets. You can copy and paste data to avoid having to enter the same information over and over.

Exam Objective: MOS Excel Core 2.1.2

1. Select the data you want to copy.
2. Click the **Copy** button, or press **Ctrl+C**.
3. Select the destination for the copied data.
4. Click the **Paste** button, or press **Ctrl+V**.

The data appears both in its original location and in the new location. The data is also still on the clipboard, in case you want to put it somewhere else as well.

Copying data by dragging

Just as you can move data by dragging, you can copy it that way as well. The only difference is that you need to hold down **Ctrl** while dragging. When you hold Ctrl and point to the border of selected data, the pointer takes the shape of an arrow with a plus sign.

Exercise: Copying data in a worksheet

My Moving and Copying is open.

Exam Objective: MOS Excel Core 2.1.2

Do This	How & Why
1. Select A7:N7.	You'll make a copy of the budget monthly headings to use on the other worksheets, which will contain budget data for years 2 and 3.
2. Click **Copy**.	The Copy button is on the Home tab, in the Clipboard group, below the Cut button. A marquee appears, telling you that the data has been copied to the clipboard.
3. Click the Year 2 worksheet tab.	You'll paste the headings on this worksheet.
4. Select A7, and press **Ctrl+V**.	The headings appear on this worksheet.
5. Activate the Year 1 worksheet.	Click its worksheet tab. Notice that the headings are still there, because you copied, rather than cut them. Also, the marquee is still showing, meaning you can paste the copied headings again.
6. Paste the copied headings onto the Year 3 worksheet. a) On the Year 3 worksheet, select A7. b) Press **Ctrl+V**.	The headings appear on this worksheet.

Do This	How & Why
7. Update the workbook.	
8. Activate the Year 1 worksheet.	Notice that the marquee is gone. When you save, the clipboard is cleared. You can also clear it by pressing Esc.
9. Copy the monthly headings to row 20 by dragging.	
a) Select A7:N7.	If necessary.
b) While holding **Ctrl**, point to the border of the selected data.	The pointer takes the shape of an arrow with a plus sign.
c) Drag the selected headings to row 20.	When you get where you want the headings, release the mouse. A copy of the headings now appears in row 20.
10. Drag a copy of the row headings in A8:A16 below the new column headings.	Select them, point to the border while holding Ctrl, and drag them down.
11. Save the workbook.	

Copying formulas

When you copy a formula that contains cell references, and then paste it into another location, Excel updates the references in the pasted formula relative to the new location.

References in a copied formula

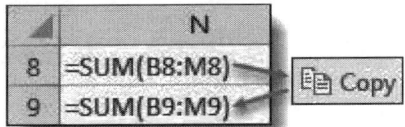

Because the formula in N8 was moved down one row, Excel increases the row numbers in the pasted formula by 1 each. So, B8 becomes B9, and M8 becomes M9. In this way, the formula continues to sum the values to the left of it. This kind of reference is called a *relative reference*.

Exercise: Copying a formula in a worksheet

My Copying and Pasting is open. You'll copy formulas and observe how references are updated when you do.

Do This	How & Why
1. In N8, enter a function to calculate the sum.	You can use AutoSum, or enter the function manually, =SUM(B8:M8).
2. Copy N8 to N9.	Select N8, copy it, select N9, and paste.
3. Select N9.	Notice that the pasted formula refers to B9:M9. These are the correct references relative to the new location of the formula. That's because Excel uses relative references by default. When you paste a copied formula, Excel updates the references in the new formula.
4. Copy N9 to N10:N15. a) Select N9. b) Copy. c) Select N10:N15. d) Paste.	You can copy from one cell and paste into a range of cells in a single paste step.
5. In B16, calculate the Jan sum.	Use the SUM() function.
6. Copy B16 to C16:N16.	Select B16, copy it, select C16:N16, and paste.
7. Select N16.	Because this cell is 12 columns to the right of the copied cell, Excel changed the references from B8:B15 to N8:N15. Column N is 12 columns over from column B.
8. Save and close the workbook.	

The completed budget

	A	B	C	D	E	F	G	H	I	J	K	L	M	N
7	Expense	Jan	Feb	Mar	Apr	May	Jun	Jul	Aug	Sep	Oct	Nov	Dec	Year Total
8	Rent	2000	2000	2000	2000	2000	2000	2000	2000	2000	2000	2000	2000	24000
9	Remodeling	10000	0	0	0	0	0	2000	0	0	0	0	0	12000
10	Legal	4000	500	0	0	0	0	0	500	0	0	0	0	5000
11	Equipment	8000	1000	0	0	0	0	0	0	0	0	0	0	9000
12	Supplies	1000	1000	1000	1000	1000	1000	1000	1000	1000	1000	1000	1000	12000
13	Advertising	3000	100	100	100	100	100	100	100	100	100	100	100	4100
14	Payroll	5000	5000	5000	5000	5000	5000	5000	5000	5000	5000	5000	5000	60000
15	Miscellaneous	800	800	800	800	800	800	800	800	800	800	800	800	9600
16	Totals:	33800	10400	8900	8900	8900	8900	10900	9400	8900	8900	8900	8900	135700

Assessment: Moving and copying data

You use the Copy command to move data. True or false?

- True
- False

Which of the following can be accomplished by dragging? Choose the one correct answer.

- Moving but not copying.
- Copying but not moving.
- Both moving and copying.

What is the keyboard shortcut to undo the most recent action?

- F1
- Ctrl+U
- Ctrl+Z
- Alt+X

To copy data by dragging, which key do you hold down?

- Shift
- Ctrl
- Alt

When you paste a copied formula, Excel updates references in the pasted formula relative to the new location.

- True
- False

Module E: Reference types

Excel uses different types of references to refer to cells and ranges either absolutely, or relatively to the location where the reference appears. The different types are useful in different situations.

You will learn:

- About the limitations of relative references
- How to enter absolute and mixed references in formulas

About reference types

Exam Objective: MOS Excel Core 4.1.1

Excel displays row numbers and column letters for your convenience in referring to locations on your worksheets. Behind the scenes, however, Excel is "thinking" about everything in terms of numbers. Here is a look at how Excel looks at a simple worksheet.

R1C1 reference style

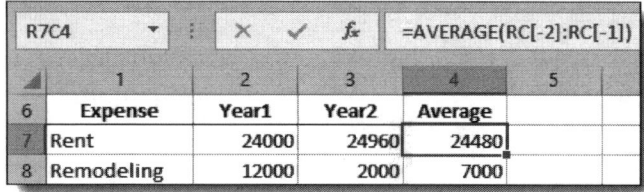

Instead of column letters, there are numbers. And in the average formula, the references look very different. What "RC[-2]" means to Excel is "this row" (R) and "2 columns to the left" (C[-2]). It might seem strange, but this is why copying formulas with relative references works. In the next figure, you're seeing both the original formula and one copied below it.

Copied relative references

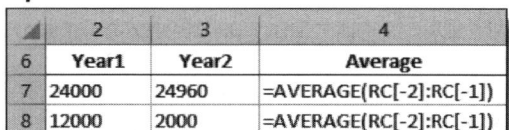

Notice that the two formulas are exactly the same. That's how Excel thinks about relative references, and that's why copying them to other locations works so well: the formula is still totalling the cells in the same row, from two columns over to one column over. It is, in fact, the same formula.

Excel also allows you to use *absolute references*, which refer to a particular location specifically, rather than in relation to the cell containing the reference. This is a better method to use when you're referring to unique values, such as commission rates, today's date, or multipliers of various kinds.

Limitations of relative references

Sometimes, you create formulas that refer, in part, to singular values in your worksheets. The classic example is a commission formula. Commissions are calculated by multiplying a sales amount by a commission rate.

A commission formula

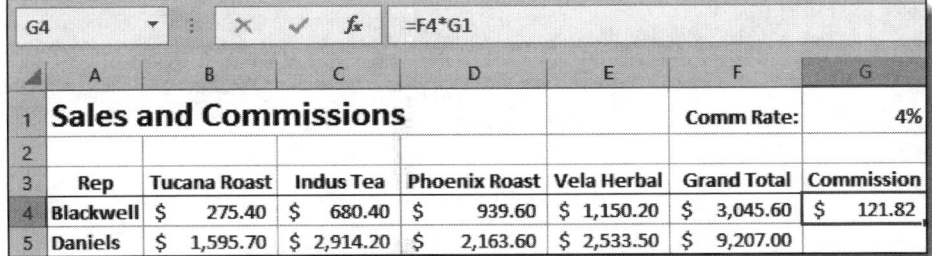

The commission is calculated by multiplying the sales total in F4 by the commission rate in G1. When the formula is copied to G5, there is a problem.

A copied commission formula

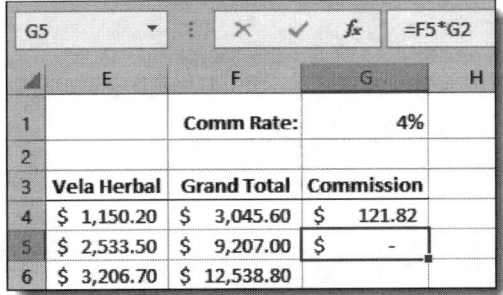

When Excel copies the relative reference to the commission rate into G5, it adjusts the reference relative to the new location (down one cell), and now refers to G2, which is blank.

Exercise: Experimenting with the limitations of relative references

In this exercise, you'll predict future years' values in a budget by using multiplier percentages. Then you'll copy those formulas to see the limitations of relative references.

 Exam Objective: MOS Excel Core 4.1.1

Do This	How & Why
1. Open Reference Types.	From the current data folder. This is a version of the café budget, projecting for five years. You're going to use the yearly modifier percentages in column I to project the future figures for rent, supplies, and payroll.
2. In C8, enter =B8*I8.	The formula calculates the projected rent for Year 2.
3. Copy C8 to D8:F8.	There is a problem with the copied formulas. D8, E8, and F8 all display 0.
4. Select D8. In the copied formula, the reference to B8 was correctly adjusted to C8. But Excel also adjusted the reference to the multiplier in I8, which is now referring to J8, a blank cell. Relative references always adjust relatively to their new location, and when you have single values like a multiplier, that's not what you want to happen. 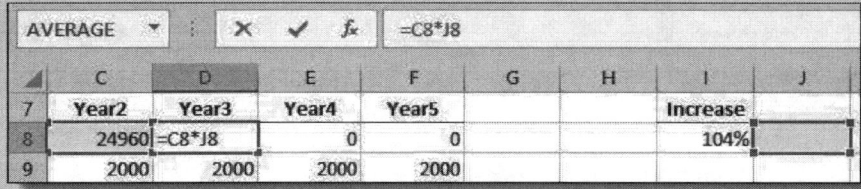	
5. Undo the pasting of the formulas and the entry of the formula in C8.	
6. Save the workbook as My Reference Types.	

How absolute references work

Absolute references are not stored in relation to the position of the formulas that contain them. They are anchored references to a specific location on a worksheet. You specify absolute references by locking the column letter and row number with a dollar sign.

 Exam Objective: MOS Excel Core 4.1.1

Absolute references in a commission formula

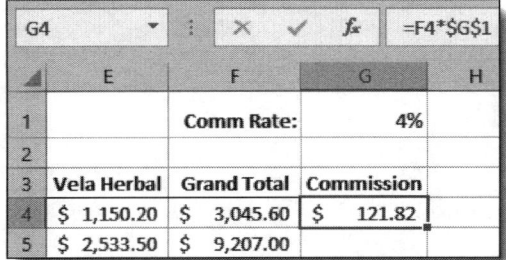

Excel looks at the absolute reference more as we do, but in R1C1 terms with column numbers instead of letters.

Absolute reference in R1C1 style

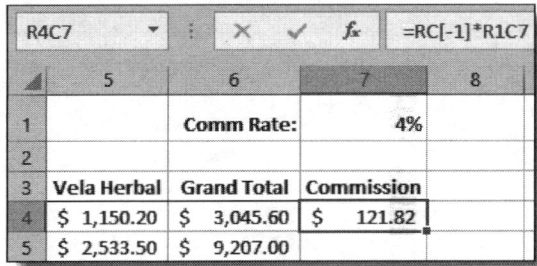

When you copy the formula down a cell, Excel sees the copied formula exactly the same way the original.

Copied relative and absolute references in R1C1

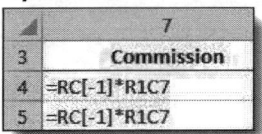

Inserting absolute references in formulas

You specify absolute references by placing a dollar sign ($) in front of column letters and row numbers.

1. Begin to create a formula.
2. Enter an absolute reference.
   - Type a dollar sign in front of the column letter and row number for the reference you want to make absolute.
   - Enter the reference, and then immediately press **F4** to switch the reference to absolute.
3. Complete and enter the formula.

Exercise: Using an absolute reference in a formula

The My Reference Types workbook is open. You'll use an absolute reference in a future year projection formula, then copy that formulas to the remaining year's projections.

Exam Objective: MOS Excel Core 4.1.1

Do This	How & Why
1. Enter the projection formula in C8.	This time, you'll use an absolute reference to the projection percentage.
a) In C8, type =B8*.	But don't press Enter yet.
b) Type $I$8.	To enter an absolute reference to cell I8.
c) Enter the formula.	
2. Copy C8 to D8:F8.	The results now look good.
3. Select D8.	In the copied formula, the relative reference to B8 was adjusted to C8, but the absolute reference to $I$8 was not changed, so the formula is correct.
4. Enter the projection formula in C12.	
a) In C12, type =B12*I12.	This time, don't type the dollar signs. And don't press Enter yet.
b) Press **F4**.	The reference to I12 changes to absolute, "$I$12."
c) Enter the formula.	
5. Copy C12 to D12:F12.	The projections for supplies are correct, because the absolute reference to I12 is not being adjusted in the copied formulas.
6. Save the workbook.	

Mixed references

There are times when you want one part of a reference, either the column letter or row number, to adjust in a copied formula while the other part does not. In those cases, you'll use *mixed references*. Really, there are four possible combinations of reference types.

- Relative: A1
- Absolute: $A$1
- Mixed: $A1
- Mixed: A$1

Inserting mixed references in formulas

You create a mixed reference by placing a dollar sign before either the column letter or the row number.

 Exam Objective: MOS Excel Core 4.1.1

1. Begin to create a formula.
2. Enter a mixed reference.
   - Type a dollar sign before either the column letter or the row number.
   - Enter the reference, and then press **F4** to cycle through the possible reference types until you get what you want.
3. Complete and enter the formula.

Exercise: Using a mixed reference in a formula

My Reference Types is open. You'll see a limitation of an absolute reference and use a mixed reference to get a better result.

 Exam Objective: MOS Excel Core 4.1.1

Do This	How & Why
1. Copy C12 to C14.	On the surface, this looks reasonable as a projection for payroll in Year 2.
2. Select C14.	The formula is using I12 as the multiplier, because the formula uses an absolute reference to it. You actually want the reference in the copied formula to be in the same column, but to a different row. This is a perfect case for using a mixed reference.
3. Undo the copied formula.	
4. Delete the Rent and Supplies projection formulas.	In C8:F8 and C12:F12. By using a mixed reference, you're going to make a single formula in C8 that can be copied to all the projections.
5. In C8, enter the projection formula.	
a) In C8, type =B8*I8.	Don't press Enter yet.
b) Press **F4**.	The reference changes to absolute, "$I$8," which is not what you want.
c) Press **F4** again.	Now, you have a mixed reference, "I$8." If you use this, when the reference is copied, the column letter will adjust, while the row number will stay fixed. That's not what you want.
d) Press **F4** again.	This is the mixed reference you want, "$I8." When this is copied, the column letter will stay fixed, but the row will adjust relatively to the new location.
e) Enter the formula.	
6. Copy C8 to D8:F8.	The formula works well when copied.
7. Copy C8 to C12:F12.	The formula also works when copied here. The mixed reference to $I8 changes relatively to the row, but the column stays fixed, giving the correct $I12 reference.
8. Copy C8 to C14:F14.	
9. Save and close the workbook.	

The completed My Reference Types workbook

	A	B	C	D	E	F
			fx	=B14*$I14		
7	Expense	Year1	Year2	Year3	Year4	Year5
8	Rent	24000	24960	25958.4	26996.736	28076.605
9	Remodeling	12000	2000	2000	2000	2000
10	Legal	5000	500	500	500	500
11	Equipment	9000	1000	1000	2000	1000
12	Supplies	12000	13200	14520	15972	17569.2
13	Advertising	4000	1000	1200	1400	1600
14	Payroll	60000	67200	75264	84295.68	94411.162
15	Miscellaneous	10000	11000	12000	13000	14000

(Cell reference C14, formula =B14*$I14)

Assessment: Reference types

All references in Excel are relative, in terms of their location. True or false?

- True
- False

Which type of reference is best for referring to a multiplier value that is in one cell on a worksheet for all formulas, no matter where the formulas are?

- Mixed
- Relative
- Absolute

Which character do you use to make a reference absolute?

- Colon (:)
- Dollar sign ($)
- Ampersand (&)
- Number sign (#)

You can use the F3 key to toggle through reference types while you enter a formula. True or false?

- True
- False

Summary: Creating worksheets

You should now know:

- How to enter numbers and text, and about how Excel handles those data types
- About the elements of Excel formulas, and how to perform calculations by entering formulas in a worksheet
- About special, named formulas called functions, and how to use them to calculate sums and averages
- How to move and copy data, either by using commands and buttons or by dragging, and about how Excel updates references in copied formulas
- About relative, absolute, and mixed references, and how and when to use each in formulas

Synthesis: Creating worksheets

In this chapter synthesis exercise, you'll create a simple sales worksheet by entering headings and data. You'll move and copy data, and then enter formulas using both relative and absolute references.

1. Open Creating Worksheets Synthesis (from the Creating Worksheets data folder).
2. On the Year 1 worksheet, enter the labels as shown.

   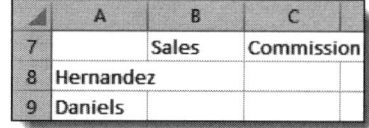

3. Widen columns A and C to fit the labels.
4. Enter the sales figures as shown.

	A	B	C
7		Sales	Commission
8	Hernandez	4000	
9	Daniels	5000	

5. Move A7:C9 down two rows.
6. Make a copy of the labels on the Year 2 and Year 3 worksheets.
7. On the Year 1 worksheet, in C10, create a commission formula using an absolute reference to the commission percentage.
8. Copy the formula in C10 to C11.
9. Use **AutoSum** to insert total functions in B12:C12.
10. Save the workbook as `My Creating Worksheets Synthesis`.

Chapter 3: Formatting

You will learn how to:

- Format text
- Format numbers
- Control alignment of data
- Apply borders and highlighting to cells and ranges
- Use styles to quickly apply various kinds of formatting in a single step

Module A: Text formatting

Text formatting in Excel is simple: you select a cell or range to which you want to apply formatting, and then click a formatting option on the ribbon. But that formatting is also powerful, with many fonts, many formats, and various other options.

You will learn:

- How to format text
- How to select multiple ranges

About text formatting

The ribbon provides the access to the most common formatting tools in the Font group.

Exam Objective: MOS Excel Core 2.2.3

The Font group on the ribbon

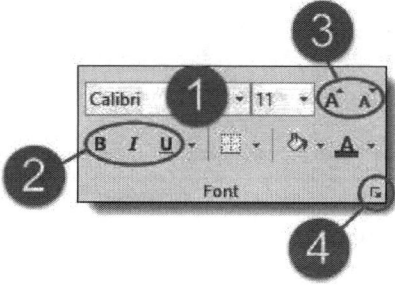

1. The *Font box* lets you specify the font of selected text.

2. These formatting buttons quickly apply bold, italic, and underline formatting to selected text.

3. The *Increase Font Size* and *Decrease Font Size* buttons.

4. The *Font Settings* button leads to the Font window, which gives you many more formatting options.

Formatting keyboard shortcuts

Command	Shortcut
Bold	**Ctrl+B**
Italic	**Ctrl+I**
Underline	**Ctrl+U**

Selecting multiple ranges

You can select more than one cell or range at the same time, so that you can perform the same action on many cells or ranges in one step. Not all commands can be applied to multiple ranges, but most formatting can be. Such ranges are called *non-contiguous ranges*.

1. Select the first cell or range.
2. While holding **Ctrl**, select any other cells or ranges you want to add to the selection.

Exercise: Formatting labels in a worksheet

Exam Objective: MOS Excel Core 2.2.5

Do This	How & Why
1. Open Formatting Text.	From the Formatting data folder. This workbook contains a list of customers, and their sales representatives, regions, and discounts.
2. Format A1 as bold, 18 pt.	
a) Select A1.	
b) Click **B**.	The Bold button is in the ribbon's Font group. "Java Tucana" is now bold.
c) In the Font Size list, click **18**.	The font size box is in the ribbon's Font group. Click the dropdown arrow to display the available sizes, which are measured in *points*, 1/72 of an inch.
3. Format A2 as italic, 14 pt.	
a) Select A2.	
b) Click **I**.	The Italic button is in the ribbon's Font group.
c) In the Font Size list, click **14**.	
4. Format A4:D4 as bold.	Select the range, then click the Bold button or press **Ctrl+B**.
5. Change the font for all the labels to **Times New Roman**.	
a) Select A1:A2.	
b) While holding **Ctrl**, select A4:D4.	This is how you select more than one range at the same time.
c) In the Font list, click **Times New Roman**.	
Continued...	

Do This	How & Why
6. Select A1.	You'll format the main title by using the Font window.
7. Click the Font Settings button.	That's the name for the little box in the lower-right of a ribbon group. 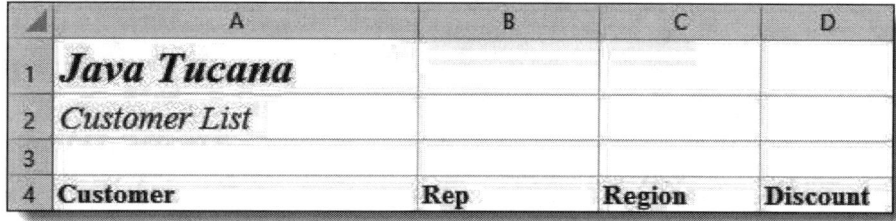 The Format Cells window opens with the Font tab active. Here, you can control everything about the font in a single place.
8. Under Font Style, click **Bold Italic**, and click **OK**.	The heading is now both bold and italic.
9. Save the workbook as My Formatting Text, and then close it.	

The formatted labels in My Formatting Text

	A	B	C	D
1	*Java Tucana*			
2	*Customer List*			
3				
4	Customer	Rep	Region	Discount

Assessment: Text formatting

To format a cell, you click the formatting button before selecting the cell you want to format. True or false?

- True
- False

Which key do you hold down to add another cell or range to a selection?

- Ctrl
- Shift
- Alt

Module B: Number formatting

Excel number formats are deceptively simple to use, but they are actually very complex. When you enter some kinds of numbers, such as percentages and dates, Excel recognizes them and automatically applies those formats. That actually changes how those numbers are stored. Other formats you need to apply manually by using either the ribbon or the Format Cells window.

You will learn how to:

- Apply currency and percentage formats
- Control decimal places
- Use the keyboard to select ranges
- Format and perform simple calculations on dates

Number formats

Here are some of the common categories of number formats in Excel.

- *Number*: Simple numbers for which you can specify the number of decimal places.
- *Currency*: Monetary values for which you can specify the particular currency (dollars or euros, for example).
- *Accounting*: Line up the currency symbols and decimals.
- *Date* and *Time*: Stored as serial numbers beginning with 1 for January 1, 1900. The decimals represent the time as a fraction of a day.
- *Percentage*: Stored as a decimal, displayed as a percentage. For example, .25 would display as 25%.
- *Fraction*: Displays a rounded fraction. You specify the accuracy.
- *Scientific*: Displays the number as a single digit and decimal to the power of 10. For example, 240 would be 2.40E+02.
- *Text*: Stores the number as text. This can be useful for codes in which you might want to look for a digit in a particular character position.
- *Special*: Has formats for things like telephone numbers and postal codes.
- *Custom*: Allows you to create your own formats, such as numbers preceded by a particular group of letters.

Applying number formats

Number formatting is simple but presents many options.

 Exam Objective: MOS Excel Core 2.2.5

1. Select the cell or range to which to apply the format.
2. Click an option in the ribbon's Number group.
   - Select a format from the Number Format list.

   - Click a format button, such as currency, percentage, or comma.

   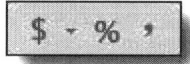

   - Click one of these buttons to increase or decrease the number of decimal places.

   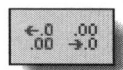

   - Click the Number Format button in the lower right of the Number group to access the Number tab of the Format Cells window.

Selecting ranges with the keyboard

You can use the keyboard to select ranges. This can be a much better way to select very large ranges.

- Hold down **Shift** while pressing arrow keys to extend the selection in any direction.
- Select a cell, point to another cell, hold down **Shift**, and click to select the range between the two cells.
- Hold down **Ctrl**, then press an arrow key repeatedly, as necessary, to select the last cell in that direction that contains data. (Or, if the next cell does not contain data, this method selects the next cell that does contain data.)
- Hold down both **Shift** and **Ctrl** to combine these techniques, quickly extending the selection to the limits of the current data.

Exercise: Formatting currency and percentages

In this exercise, you'll open a workbook with sales information and format currency and percentage values.

 Exam Objective: MOS Excel Core 2.2.5

Do This	How & Why
1. Open Formatting Numbers.	From the Formatting data folder. The first worksheet contains sales information for customers buying two kinds of coffees (Tucana Roast and Phoenix Roast), and two teas (Indus Tea and Vela Herbal).
2. Format the sales values as currency.	

Do This	How & Why
a) Select B8:F53.	Try using the keyboard. Select B8, then while holding Shift, use the right arrow to extend the selection to F8. Now hold down both Ctrl and Shift, and press the down arrow key once to extend the selection to the bottom of the data in row 53.
b) Click [$].	In the Number group. The default accounting format has a dollar sign on the far left of the cell, two decimal places, and a comma separator for thousands. You can control all of that. Grand Total $ 4,360.50 $ 2,509.20
3. Select B8:F53, then click [.00→.0] twice.	Now the values show no decimal places.
4. Select B8.	While the cell displays 975, which is rounded, if you look at the formula bar you'll see that the stored value has not been changed. Number formats do not change their underlying values; they change only how those values appear.
5. Select G8.	This cell calculates how much of the sales for Accounts now are coffee sales (the values for Tucana Roast and Phoenix Roast). Numbers in this column should appear as percentages.
6. Format G8:H53 as percent. a) Select G8:H53. b) Click [%].	The values are now displayed as percentages.
7. Increase the decimal places for the percentages to 1. a) Select G8:H53. b) Click [←.0/.00].	The percentages now show one decimal place.
8. Save the workbook as My Formatting Numbers.	

The formatted Customer Sales worksheet

	B	C	D	E	F	G	H
7	Tucana Roast	Indus Tea	Phoenix Roast	Vela Herbal	Grand Total	Coffee %	Tea %
8	$ 975	$ 975	$ 872	$ 1,539	$ 4,361	42.4%	57.6%
9	$ 811	$ 413	$ 765	$ 520	$ 2,509	62.8%	37.2%
10	$ 1,328	$ 745	$ 518	$ 1,442	$ 4,034	45.8%	54.2%
11	$ 437	$ 907	$ 826	$ 243	$ 2,414	52.3%	47.7%
12	$ 761	$ 421	$ 648	$ 713	$ 2,543	55.4%	44.6%

Dates

You can enter dates in various ways, and Excel recognizes that what you've entered is a date. These are some examples of date formats that Excel recognizes.

- mm/dd/yy, for example, 01/01/2016
- mmm dd, for example, Jan 01
- dd-mmm, for example, 01-Jan

When you enter a date in a recognized format, Excel stores it as a serial number, starting with the number 1 for January 1, 1900, 2 for January 2, 1900, and so on. Because dates are stored in this way, you can perform calculations on them, such as figuring out how many days there are between two dates. Excel also has many functions for working with dates, all of which work because of the serial number system.

Exercise: Experimenting with date formats

My Formatting Numbers is open. You'll format dates several ways and perform a calculation on a date to understand how serial number storage of dates works.

Do This	How & Why
1. Activate the Employees worksheet.	This worksheet contains a list of employees, their departments, and hire dates.
2. In D3, enter today's date.	Enter it in mm/dd/yy format, for example, "01/01/16" for January 1, 2016. Excel recognizes the date, and displays it in a slightly different format. *Today's Date:* 1/1/2016
3. Select D8:D507.	Select D8, hold down **Shift** and **Ctrl**, and press the down arrow key. You'll change the date format for these numbers.
4. In the Number Format list, click **General**.	To format the numbers exactly as Excel sees them. Excel stores numbers as serial numbers. Can you think why that would be?
5. Format D8:D507 as **Long Date**.	Select the range if necessary, then click Long Date (in the Number Format list). Date of Hire Saturday, February 3, 2001 Tuesday, December 18, 1984 Wednesday, December 11, 2013 Monday, August 5, 2013 Wednesday, September 25, 1985
6. Observe the options for date formats. a) Select D8:D507.	

Do This	How & Why
b) Display the Format Cells window.	In the lower-right corner of the ribbon's Number group, click the Number Format button.
c) Click the **Number** tab and click the **Date** category.	If necessary. You can scroll through the Type list to see all the ways Excel can display a date.
d) Click **Cancel**.	
7. Select E8.	You'll enter a formula to calculate Katrice Abeita's days of service with the company.
8. Enter =$D$3-D8.	You need to use the absolute reference to today's date because that reference should not change when you copy the formula. Excel shows you the number of days between the two dates.
9. Copy E8 to E9:E507.	Select E8 and copy it. To select E9:E507, select E9, then scroll to view E507, and while holding **Shift**, click E507. Then paste the copied cell.
10. Save and close the workbook.	

The completed Employees worksheet

	A	B	C	D	E
1					
2					
3	JAVA TUCANA		Today's Date:	1/1/2016	
4					
5	Employee List with Dates of Hire				
6					
7	First	Last	Dept	Date of Hire	Service
8	Katrice	Abeita	Marketing	Saturday, February 3, 2001	5445
9	Ezequiel	Abels	Customer Service	Tuesday, December 18, 1984	11336
10	Amalia	Adcox	Customer Service	Wednesday, December 11, 2013	751
11	Irina	Alaimo	Marketing	Monday, August 5, 2013	879
12	Renetta	Albrecht	Retail Sales	Wednesday, September 25, 1985	11055

Cell reference: E8, formula: =$D$3-D8

Assessment: Number formatting

When you change a number format, you change the underlying data. True or false?

- True
- False

Which of the following is not a category of Excel number formats?

- Currency
- Exponent
- Percentage
- Date

Which key enables you to extend a selection by using the arrow keys?

- Shift
- Ctrl
- Alt

How are dates stored in Excel?

- As two pieces of data, a combination of a date and a time
- In the format in which you enter them
- As serial numbers

Module C: Alignment

You can align cell contents vertically or horizontally. You can also wrap text within cells, or merge cells to treat larger ranges as a single cell.

You will learn how to:

- Align cell contents vertically and horizontally
- Wrap text within a cell
- Merge the contents of multiple cells

Horizontal and vertical alignment

Because cells are boxes, you can align their contents both vertically (top, middle, or bottom) and horizontally (left, center, or right), resulting in nine combinations.

	Left	Center	Right
Top	Text	Text	Text
Middle	Text	Text	Text
Botton	Text	Text	Text

Excel actually gives you even more possibilities, including the ability to indent cell contents and to orient text diagonally or vertically.

Aligning cell contents

You set alignment by selecting a cell, and then clicking an Alignment button.

 Exam Objective: MOS Excel Core 2.2.2

Alignment buttons

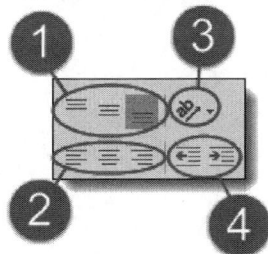

① *Vertical alignment* possibilities include top, middle, and bottom.

② *Horizontal alignment* possibilities include left, center, and right.

③ *Orientation* lets you make text run diagonally or vertically.

④ *Indent* buttons let you increase or decrease the margin between the data and the cell border.

Exercise: Aligning text in a worksheet

Exam Objective: MOS Excel Core 2.2.2

Do This	How & Why
1. Open Alignment.	From the Formatting data folder. This workbook contains info about Java Tucana customers.
2. Select A5, and observe the horizontal alignment buttons.	None are selected by default. But text, by default, is left-aligned, as this worksheet title is.
3. Center the column labels. a) Select A8:E8. b) Click [icon].	The center button. Now, the column headings are centered.
4. Select D9:D54.	These are the discount percentages. Again, no horizontal alignment has been set, but because these are numbers, the default is that they are right-aligned.
5. Center the selected range.	
6. Save the workbook as My Alignment.	

Wrapping text

When you wrap text, it continues on the next line within a cell, rather than spilling over or being cut off. This is very useful for columns of information that contain notes, for example.

Exam Objective: MOS Excel Core 2.2.4

1. Select the cell or range containing the text you want to wrap.
2. In the Alignment group of the ribbon, click **Wrap Text**.

Setting vertical alignment

To set vertical alignment, select the cell or range, and then click one of the vertical alignment buttons: Top, Middle, or Bottom.

Exercise: Wrapping text in a notes column

My Alignment is open.

 Exam Objective: MOS Excel Core 2.2.4

Do This	How & Why
1. Select column E.	Click its heading. You'll wrap the text in this column.
2. Click **Wrap Text**.	The button is in the Alignment group on the ribbon. The notes now wrap in the cells in the column. | Region	Discount	Notes | |---|---|---| | International | 10% | Send invoices by mail only; contact to renegotiate discount rate. | | US | 10% | | | US | 20% | Contact to regneotiate discount rate. |
3. Observe the data in columns A:D.	All of the data is aligned to the bottoms of the cells. Often, it looks better to align at the top when you have data wrapping in a table.
4. Select A9:E54.	To select the range quickly, select A9, hold down **Ctrl** and **Shift**, press the right arrow key and then the down arrow key. You'll top-align all of the data in the table.
5. Click ▤ .	The Top Align button is in the ribbon's Alignment group. Now, all the data in the table is top-aligned.
6. Save the workbook.	

The customer data top-aligned, with wrapped notes

Customer	Rep	Region	Discount	Notes
Accounts Now	McCanney	International	10%	Send invoices by mail only; contact to renegotiate discount rate.
Award Sportswear	Westlein	US	10%	
Blastera	Westlein	US	20%	Contact to regneotiate discount rate.
BlazerFire	Daniels	US	30%	
Brocadero	Westlein	US	20%	Send invoices by mail only.

Merging cell data

You can merge cells to make data appear over multiple columns or next to multiple rows. This is particularly useful for headings that apply to multiple columns (or entire tables), or for notes that apply to multiple rows.

After you merge cells, some Excel operations don't work on those cells. It's best to keep merging to a minimum.

Merging cells

You merge cells by selecting them and then clicking a merge option in the ribbon's Alignment group. There are several options:

Exam Objective: MOS Excel Core 2.2.1

- **Merge & Center.**
    Merges the selected cells and centers the contents over the merged columns as a whole.
    Merged and centered

	A	B	C	D	E
5		Customer List			
6		With Sales Rep and Region			
7					
8	Customer	Rep	Region	Discount	Notes
9	Accounts Now	McCanney	International	10%	Send invoices by mail only; contact to renegotiate discount rate.
10	Award Sportswear	Westlein	US	10%	
11	Blastera	Westlein	US	20%	Contact to regneotiate discount rate.

- **Merge Across.**
    Merges across, but does not center.
    Merged across

	A	B	C	D	E
5	Customer List				
6	With Sales Rep and Region				
7					
8	Customer	Rep	Region	Discount	Notes
9	Accounts Now	McCanney	International	10%	Send invoices by mail only; contact to renegotiate discount rate.
10	Award Sportswear	Westlein	US	10%	
11	Blastera	Westlein	US	20%	Contact to regneotiate discount rate.

- **Merge Cells.**
    Merges selected cells. Can be used for merging vertically.
- **Unmerge Cells.**
    Unmerges selected cells.

Exercise: Merging headings and note cells

My Alignment is open.

 Exam Objective: MOS Excel Core 2.2.1

Do This	How & Why
1. Select A5:E5.	You'll make the label centered over the entire table.
2. Click **Merge & Center**.	In the Alignment group.
3. Merge A6 over columns A:E.	Select A6:E6, then click Merge & Center.
4. Select E13:E14.	You want this note to apply to both Brocadero and Callisure, so you'll merge the two cells.
5. In the Merge list, click **Merge Cells**.	Click the dropdown arrow, then click the button.
6. Decrease the height of row 13.	Double-click the border between rows 13 and 14. Now, it looks like the note applies to both rows.
7. Save and close the workbook.	

Complete My Alignment workbook with merges cells

Customer List				
With Sales Rep and Region				
Customer	Rep	Region	Discount	Notes
Accounts Now	McCanney	International	10%	Send invoices by mail only; contact to renegotiate discount rate.
Award Sportswear	Westlein	US	10%	
Blastera	Westlein	US	20%	Contact to regneotiate discount rate.
BlazerFire	Daniels	US	30%	
Brocadero	Westlein	US	20%	Send invoices by mail only.
Callinsure	Patterson	US	20%	

Assessment: Alignment

You can align cell contents:

- Horizontally but not vertically.
- Vertically but not horizontally.
- Both vertically and horizontally.

You cannot wrap text in Excel. True or false?

- True.
- False.

The Merge & Center command is most useful for which of the following?

- Data values.
- Column headings.
- Overall worksheet headings and subheadings.

Module D: Borders and highlighting

You can apply borders to make your worksheets easier to read. For example, borders below column labels can help distinguish the labels from the data below, and horizontal borders can help the eye scan along rows of data.

You will learn how to:

- Apply borders to cells and ranges
- Apply highlighting, or fill colors, to cells and ranges

Applying borders

Excel gives you many ways to apply borders to a selected cell or range.

- In the Font group, display the Borders menu, and then click the type of border you want.
    You can place borders on any side of the selection, on all sides, or as a grid, as well as choose other combinations and thicknesses.

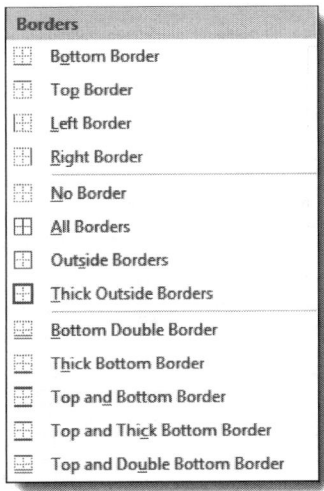

- Draw borders.
    To do this, click Draw Border in the Borders menu. The mouse pointer takes the shape of a pencil, and you can simply click where you want borders to appear. When you're done, press **Esc**.
- Use the Borders tab of the Format Cells window.
    To do this, at the bottom of the Borders menu, click **More Borders**. This gives you enormous control over the style, weight, and placement of borders.

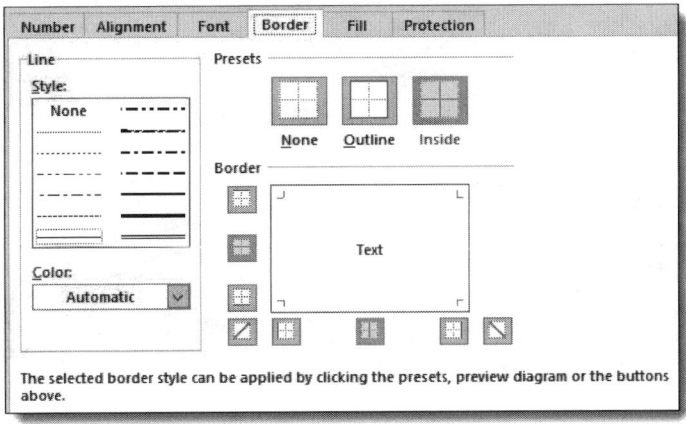

Highlighting ranges

Another way to call attention to a cell or range is to highlight it by applying a fill color.

1. Select the range to which you want to apply a fill color.
2. In the Font group, click the Fill Color dropdown arrow.
   A palette of fill colors appears.

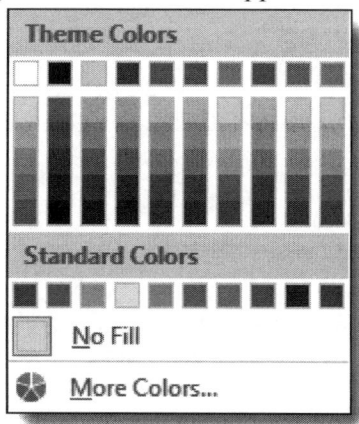

3. Click the color you want, or click **More Colors** to get more color options.

Exercise: Applying borders and highlighting to a worksheet

Do This	How & Why
1. Open Borders.	From the Formatting data folder. This workbook contains sales information by sales representative and product.
2. Apply a bottom border to the column headings. a) Select A7:F7. b) Click ▦.	 The bottom border button is in the Font group's Borders menu.
c) Select any cell.	So you can see the border below the headings.
3. Apply a grid of borders to the data. a) Select A8:F17. b) In the Borders menu, click **All Borders**.	

Do This	How & Why
c) Select any cell.	To view the grid of borders.
4. Draw a heavy border below the headings.	
a) In the Borders menu, click **Line Style**, then the heavy line.	Notice that the pointer takes the shape of a pencil. 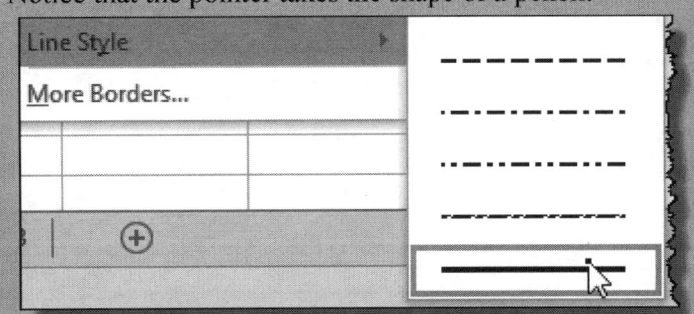
b) Drag to draw a border under the headings.	
c) Press **Esc**.	The pointer again takes the default shape.
5. Place a heavy border below row 17.	
a) Select A17:F17.	
b) In the Borders menu, click **More Borders**.	To display the Format Cells window, where you can control every aspect of the borders.
c) In the Style list, click a heavy line.	
d) In the Border area, click the bottom of the preview. It should look like this. 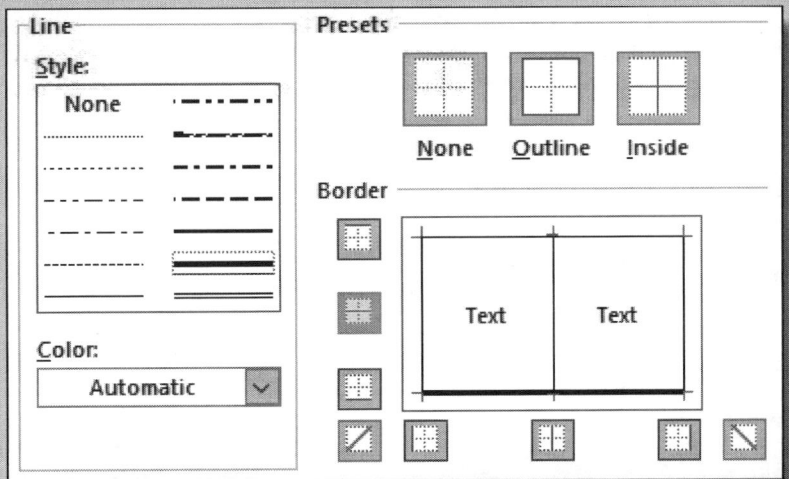	
e) Click **OK**.	The border appears at the bottom of the row.
Continued...	

Do This	How & Why
6. Highlight Lloyd's row. a) Select A12:F12. b) Click the Fill Color dropdown, then click a color you like. c) Select any cell. 7. Save the workbook as My Borders, then close it.	You want to highlight the rep with the highest sales total. The Fill Color button is in the Font group. So you can see the highlighting.

The completed My Borders workbook

Rep	Tucana Roast	Indus Tea	Phoenix Roast	Vela Herbal	Total
Blackwell	$ 275.40	$ 680.40	$ 939.60	$ 1,150.20	$ 3,045.60
Daniels	$ 1,595.70	$ 2,914.20	$ 2,163.60	$ 2,533.50	$ 9,207.00
Franklin	$ 3,938.40	$ 2,623.50	$ 2,770.20	$ 3,206.70	$ 12,538.80
Hernandez	$ 3,324.60	$ 2,852.10	$ 3,851.10	$ 5,571.90	$ 15,599.70
Lloyd	$ 5,071.50	$ 6,271.20	$ 5,890.50	$ 6,158.70	$ 23,391.90
McCanney	$ 3,618.00	$ 4,826.70	$ 4,645.80	$ 6,976.80	$ 20,067.30
Patterson	$ 1,843.20	$ 1,399.50	$ 1,585.80	$ 2,284.20	$ 7,112.70
Sanchez	$ 4,054.50	$ 2,261.70	$ 3,958.20	$ 2,630.70	$ 12,905.10
Schiller	$ 4,765.50	$ 4,755.60	$ 4,764.60	$ 4,954.50	$ 19,240.20
Westlein	$ 4,488.30	$ 4,164.30	$ 3,832.20	$ 4,361.40	$ 16,846.20
Total:	$ 32,975.10	$ 32,749.20	$ 34,401.60	$39,828.60	$139,954.50

Assessment: Borders

Which of the following are ways to apply borders to a cell or range? Choose all that apply.

- Use buttons in the Borders menu.
- Double-click cell borders.
- Use the Draw Border feature.
- Use the Borders tab of the Format Cells window.

Thin and thick lines are the only border style options. True or false?

- True.
- False.

Module E: Styles and themes

A style is a combination of formats that you apply in a single step. For example, you might have a style that sets the font and size, number format, shading, and borders for a cell. Excel has many built-in-styles, and you can also define your own. Themes define a set of colors, fonts, and effects that go together to make your workbooks look good. You can choose existing themes or customize them.

You will learn:

- How to apply cell styles to cells and ranges
- How to clear formats from a selected cell or range
- How to use table styles to quickly format an entire table of data
- About themes and how to change and customize them.

Applying cell styles

Cell styles apply to the selected cell or range and apply one set of formats to all cells in the selection.

Exam Objective: MOS Excel Core 2.3.2

1. Select a cell or range.
2. In the Home ribbon's Styles group:
   - If you see a gallery of styles, click its **More** arrow.
   - If you see the **Cell Styles** button, click that. Your screen resolution and window size determines how much you see on the ribbon.

   There are many choices in the *Style gallery*. You can apply styles that have particular meanings (good, bad, neutral, data, and model), ones that apply to headings, or styles that are grouped by themes.

   The Style gallery

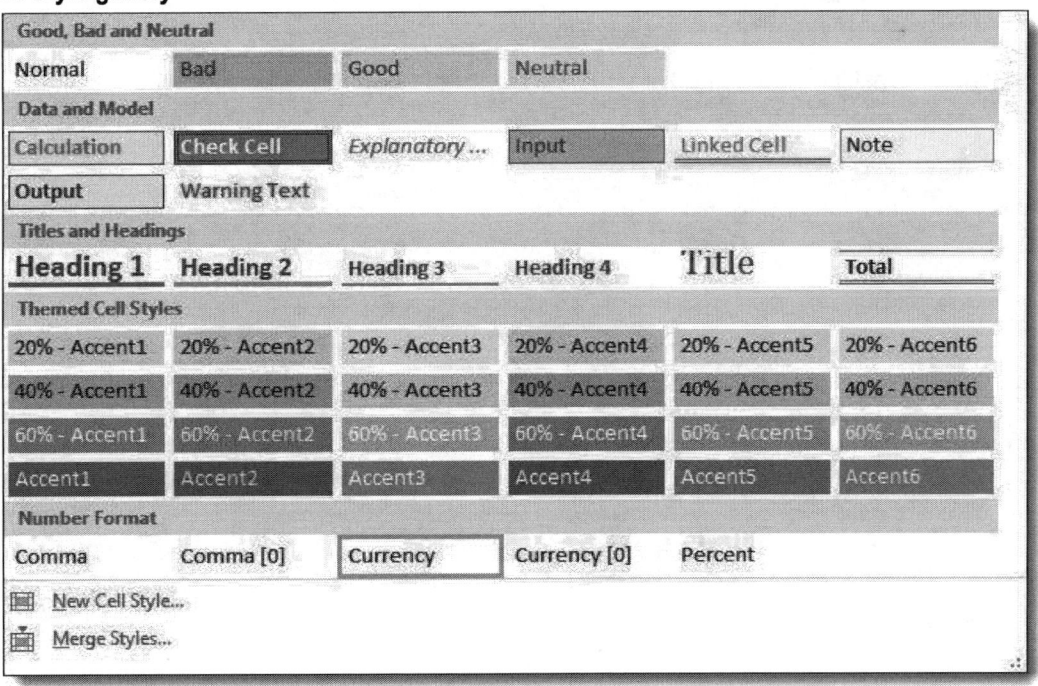

3. Click a style.

Clearing formats

To clear formats from a selection, in the Editing group, click the dropdown arrow for the Clear command, then click **Clear Formats**.

Applying table styles

One of the best time-saving features in Excel is *table styles*. By using the Format as Table command, you can format entire tables in a single step. Excel takes care of headings and total rows for you.

Exam Objective: MOS Excel Core 3.2.1

1. Select the table you want to format.
    You can also select a single cell within the table.
2. Click **Format as Table**.
    The Table Style gallery provides a wide variety of table formatting options.
    The Table Style gallery

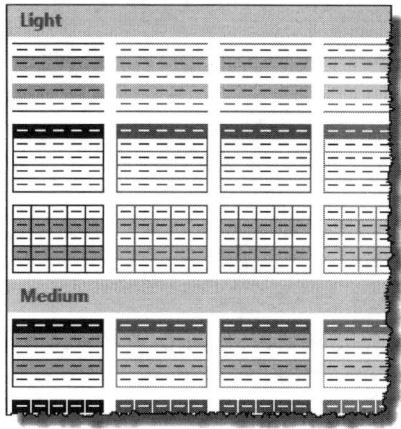

3. Click a table style.
    To display the Format as Table window, which prompts you to enter or confirm the range of the selection. You're also asked to specify whether the table has headers.
4. Modify the range if necessary, then click **OK**.

The entire table is formatted—headings as headings, totals as totals. After you format a range as a table in this way, the gallery has a preview function that allows you to hover the pointer over the styles and see how they look on the table. Note that when you format a range as a table, Excel gives you access to various other table features.

Creating cell styles

If you have formatted a cell in a particular way, and want to use that formatting on other cells and ranges, you can create your own cell styles.

Exam Objective: MOS Excel Expert 2.3.2

1. Format a cell in the way you want to use for a style.
2. Display the Style Gallery (click its More arrow), and then click **New Cell Style** at the bottom of the gallery.
    To display the Style window.

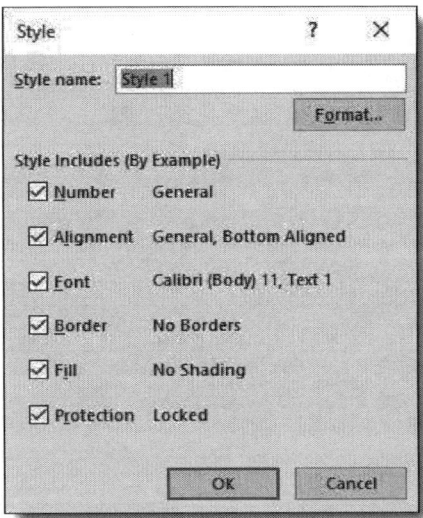

3. Set the options you want.
   - Type a name in the Style name box.
   - Click style elements to include or not include them (number formatting, alignment, and so on).
   - To change the formatting from that of the selected cell, click the **Format** button.
4. Click **OK**.

The new style appears in the Style gallery, and you can apply it as you would any other style.

Exercise: Applying cell and table styles to a worksheet

In this exercise, you'll quickly format headings and other cells by using cell styles, then clear that formatting and format a table in a single step by using table styles.

 Exam Objective: MOS Excel Core 2.3.2 and Expert 3.2.1

Do This	How & Why
1. Open Styles.	From the Formatting data folder.
2. Format the worksheet title using a style. a) Select A5.	
b) Click **Cell Styles**.	If you don't see the Cell Styles button, click the More arrow in the styles gallery on the ribbon. The Styles gallery appears.
c) Click **Title**.	Under Title and Headings. The title is now larger, bold, in a different font, and in a different color.
3. Format the worksheet headings using a style. a) Select A7:F7. Continued...	

Do This	How & Why
b) In the Styles gallery, click **Heading 3**.	The headings change color, are bold, and have a border below.
c) Observe the Styles group.	Notice that Excel is showing a group of style choices that might make sense with the choice you just made. The ribbon is often *context-sensitive* in this way. And the styles go together because they are part of a *theme*. Note that if you have a smaller screen or the Excel window is not maximized, you might not see styles on the ribbon without clicking the Cell Styles button.
4. Use a style to format the values as currency with no decimal places.	
a) Select B8:F18.	
b) In the Styles gallery, click **Currency (0)**.	It's at the bottom, under Number Format.
5. Format the totals row.	
a) Select A18:F18.	
b) Apply the **Total** style.	Select **Total** from the gallery.

6. Select any cell.

   You've quickly formatted the table. But there's an even quicker way.

Sales by Representative					
Rep	Tucana Roast	Indus Tea	Phoenix Roast	Vela Herbal	Total
Blackwell	$ 275	$ 680	$ 940	$ 1,150	$ 3,046
Daniels	$ 1,596	$ 2,914	$ 2,164	$ 2,534	$ 9,207
Franklin	$ 3,938	$ 2,624	$ 2,770	$ 3,207	$ 12,539
Hernandez	$ 3,325	$ 2,852	$ 3,851	$ 5,572	$ 15,600
Lloyd	$ 5,072	$ 6,271	$ 5,891	$ 6,159	$ 23,392
McCanney	$ 3,618	$ 4,827	$ 4,646	$ 6,977	$ 20,067
Patterson	$ 1,843	$ 1,400	$ 1,586	$ 2,284	$ 7,113
Sanchez	$ 4,055	$ 2,262	$ 3,958	$ 2,631	$ 12,905
Schiller	$ 4,766	$ 4,756	$ 4,765	$ 4,955	$ 19,240
Westlein	$ 4,488	$ 4,164	$ 3,832	$ 4,361	$ 16,846
Total:	$ 32,975	$ 32,749	$ 34,402	$ 39,829	$ 139,955

7. Clear the formats from the table.

   a) Select A7:F18.

Do This	How & Why
b) In the Editing group, display the **Clear** menu, then click **Clear Formats**.	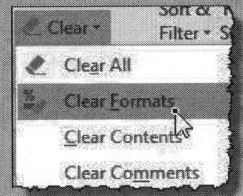
	All formatting is removed from the entire selected range.
8. Format the range using a table style.	
a) Select A7:F18.	If necessary.
b) Click **Format as Table**.	To display the Table Style gallery. There are many options.
c) Click a medium style.	A window appears giving you the chance to modify the table selection. Note that "My table has headers" is checked.
d) Click **OK**, then select any cell.	It's not perfect. You might, for example, want to format the values as currency now. But it does so much of the formatting work for you. Formatting as a table also gives you access to Excel's Table Tools, which are covered in another course.
9. Preview other table styles.	
a) Click anywhere in the table.	
b) Display the Table Style gallery.	
c) Hover over any format.	When you do, you can see how that format would look on the table.
d) Press **Esc**.	
10. Save the workbook as `My Styles`.	

The completed My Styles worksheet.

Rep	Tucana Roast	Indus Tea	Phoenix Roast	Vela Herbal	Total
Blackwell	275.4	680.4	939.6	1150.2	3045.6
Daniels	1595.7	2914.2	2163.6	2533.5	9207
Franklin	3938.4	2623.5	2770.2	3206.7	12538.8
Hernandez	3324.6	2852.1	3851.1	5571.9	15599.7
Lloyd	5071.5	6271.2	5890.5	6158.7	23391.9
McCanney	3618	4826.7	4645.8	6976.8	20067.3
Patterson	1843.2	1399.5	1585.8	2284.2	7112.7
Sanchez	4054.5	2261.7	3958.2	2630.7	12905.1
Schiller	4765.5	4755.6	4764.6	4954.5	19240.2
Westlein	4488.3	4164.3	3832.2	4361.4	16846.2
Total:	32975.1	32749.2	34401.6	39828.6	139954.5

Themes

Themes are groups of colors, fonts, and effects that govern your style choices in a workbook. There is a default theme, but you can also change to other themes, or customize a theme to suit your taste and needs.

Exam Objective: MOS Excel Expert 2.3.3

You change themes by using the Themes button on the Page Layout tab of the ribbon. The Themes group also has menus in which you can change colors, fonts, or effects for the current theme.

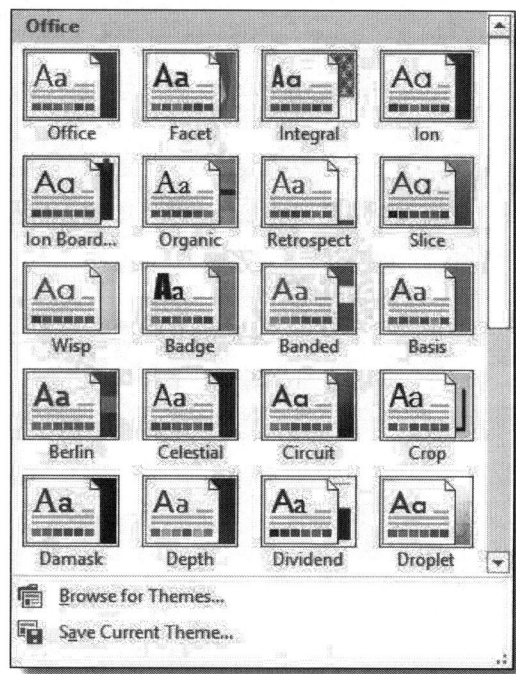

Exercise: Experimenting with themes

My Styles is open.

Exam Objective: MOS Excel Expert 2.3.3

Do This	How & Why
1. Observe the Themes group.	On the Page Layout tab of the ribbon. Themes are coordinated sets of colors, fonts, and effects that govern the available styles.
2. Click **Themes**.	To display the Themes gallery.
3. Experiment with how various themes affect the styles of the table.	
a) Hover over various themes in the Themes gallery.	As you do, the table styles change to reflect the theme. Note that if you start with a black and white (grayscale) style, themes and colors will not affect the table color.

Do This	How & Why
b) Click a theme you like.	Notice that all of the styled elements change: the title, the headings, the totals, and more.
4. In the Themes group, click **Colors**.	To display the Colors gallery. A theme comprises colors, fonts, and effects, but you can use these buttons to modify those elements of a theme individually.
5. Click **Customize Colors**.	In the Colors gallery. To display the Create New Theme Colors window. Here, you can customize theme colors down to the individual style level.
6. Click **Cancel**.	
7. Save and close the workbook.	

Assessment: Styles and themes

You have to create a style before using one. True or false?

- True
- False

Which of the following can a style include? Choose all that apply.

- Number format
- Formulas
- Text format
- Borders
- Shading

Which of the following statements is most accurate? Choose only one.

- Table styles never include headings.
- Table styles may or may not include headings.
- Table styles always include headings.

Which elements of a theme can you control individually? Choose all that apply.

- Borders
- Font
- Number formats
- Colors
- Effects

Summary: Formatting

You should now know:

- How to apply text formatting to single cells, ranges, and multiple ranges
- How to apply number formats to values, about how Excel handles dates, and how to apply date formats
- How to align cell contents vertically and horizontally, how to wrap text within a cell, and how to merge multiple cells into a single cell
- How to apply borders to cells and ranges in your worksheets by using commands, by drawing, and by using the Border tab of the Format Cells window; and how to apply fill colors to highlight cells and ranges
- About styles and how to apply them to cells, ranges, and tables to quickly format your worksheets; and about themes and how to use them to control the available style options, as well as how to change and customize themes

Synthesis: Formatting

In this chapter synthesis exercise, you'll format a table of data by applying text and number formatting, borders, and alignment. Then, you'll format a similar table quickly using styles.

1. Open Formatting Synthesis.
    From the Formatting data folder.
2. In the Formatting worksheet, format the title in A5 as Calibri, bold, 24 pt, and center it over the entire table.
3. Format the subtitle in A6 as Calibri, italic, 18 pt, and center it over the entire table.
4. Make the column headings bold and centered, and place a thick border below them.
5. Place a double border above the totals row.
6. Format the relevant values as currency with no decimal places.
7. Format the values in column G as percentages.
8. Wrap the text in column I.
9. Top-align the table data.
10. Enter the current date in I3, then format it as **Long Date**.
11. Save the workbook as `My Formatting Synthesis`.
12. On the Styles worksheet, experiment with cell and table styles.
13. With the Styles worksheet active, experiment with changing theme and theme components.
14. Update and close the workbook.

The completed Formatting Synthesis worksheet

Sample Café Opening Budget
Years 1-5

Expense	Year1	Year2	Year3	Year4	Year5	Inc. %	Total	Notes
Rent	$ 24,000	$ 24,000	$ 24,000	$ 25,200	$ 25,200	105%	$ 122,400	Rent agreement has escalator in year 4
Remodeling	$ 12,000	$ 2,000	$ 2,000	$ 2,000	$ 2,000		$ 20,000	Most of the expense in year 1
Legal	$ 5,000	$ 500	$ 500	$ 500	$ 500		$ 7,000	Most of the expense in year 1
Equipment	$ 9,000	$ 1,000	$ 1,000	$ 2,000	$ 1,000		$ 14,000	Most of the expense in year 1
Supplies	$ 12,000	$ 13,200	$ 14,520	$ 15,972	$ 17,569	110%	$ 73,261	Will rise proportionally with sales
Advertising	$ 4,000	$ 1,000	$ 1,200	$ 1,400	$ 1,600		$ 9,200	Intermittent campaigns after initial splash
Payroll	$ 60,000	$ 69,000	$ 79,350	$ 91,253	$104,940	115%	$ 404,543	Hiring part time workers and giving more hours as necessary
Miscellaneous	$ 10,000	$ 11,000	$ 12,100	$ 13,310	$ 14,641	110%	$ 61,051	
Total	$136,000	$121,700	$134,670	$151,635	$167,451		$ 711,455	

Chapter 4: Manipulating data

You will learn:

- How to use various techniques to enter similar data quickly
- How to paste parts of cell data and formats
- How to insert, delete, and hide cells, ranges, and worksheets

Module A: Data entry shortcuts

Often, you'll want to use the same or similar data along a row or down a column. For example, you might want a series of months or years as column headings. Or you might just want the same value in one cell as in the one above it. For the same data, you can copy and paste, but Excel has shortcuts as well as tools for entering series that are very convenient.

You will learn how to:

- Use Fill commands to copy data to adjacent cells
- Use Auto Fill to copy data or extend series
- Find and replace data

Fill and Auto Fill

Fill commands and Auto Fill are very useful shortcuts for entering data.

- *Fill commands* allow you to copy a value into the adjacent cells, either down, up, to the right, or to the left.
- *Auto Fill* allows you to copy data or to extend series by dragging.

When you use Auto Fill, Excel guesses at your intended result. If the result isn't what you want, you can use the Auto Fill Options button to change how Excel performs the fill operation.

Using Fill commands

You can copy data to an adjacent cell or cells in a single step by using Fill commands. There are two ways to use them.

- Select both the cell containing the data to be copied and the range to which you want to copy it, click **Fill**, and choose the appropriate fill command.
    Here, you use **Fill Down**, or press **Ctrl+D**.

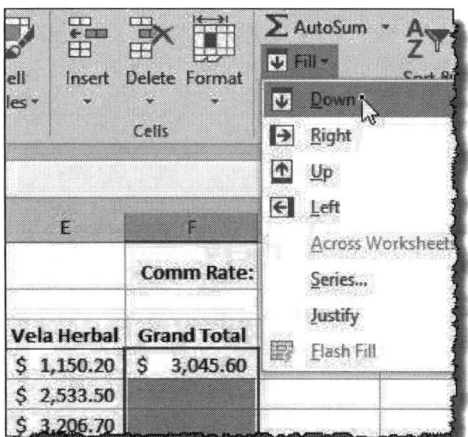

- Select the cell next to the cell containing the data you want to copy, click **Fill**, then click the appropriate fill command.
    Use the direction that describes the direction of the copy. For example, here you'd use **Fill Right** or press **Ctrl+R**.

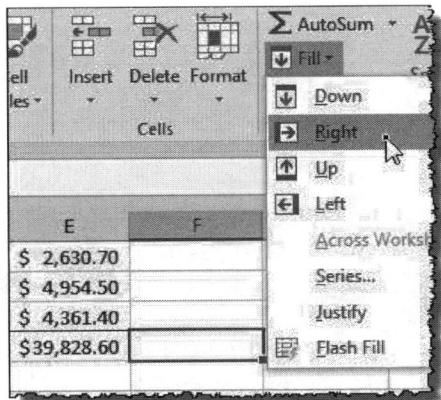

Using Auto Fill

Select a cell or range, and then drag its *fill handle* to either copy the data it contains or extend a series. How Excel fills the range to which you drag depends on what you've selected.

Exam Objective: MOS Excel Core 2.1.2 and Expert 2.1.4

1. Select a cell containing a value you want to copy, or the first value or first two values in a series you want to extend.

   Excel recognizes certain kinds of series from a single value. For example, if you start with a month name or abbreviation, or with "Qtr1" or "Year1," Excel knows you want to extend the series. In some cases, you need to enter the first two values. For example, to extend a series of years, you have to enter the first two years.

2. Drag the fill handle in the direction you want to copy or extend.

   As you drag, Excel shows you the values it will fill when you let go.

   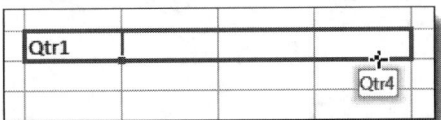

3. Click the **Auto Fill Options** button to change how Excel handles the fill operation:
   - As a copy
   - As a series
   - With or without formatting

   Note that the specific Auto Fill options change, depending on context.

Exercise: Using Fill and Auto Fill to quickly complete a worksheet

In this exercise, you'll complete a budget worksheet quickly by using Fill commands and Auto Fill. You'll also experiment with how Excel handles a series according to its first value.

Exam Objective: MOS Excel Core 2.1.3 and Expert 2.1.4

Do This	How & Why
1. Open Data Entry.	From the Manipulating Data folder. This workbook contains the beginnings of a 12-month operating budget for a café.
2. Copy the rent figures to the rest of the budget.	
a) Select B8:M8.	
b) In the Editing group, click **Fill**, then click **Right**.	The value is copied to the entire range.
3. Copy the rest of the budget values and total formulas throughout the range.	
a) Select B9:M13.	
b) Press **Ctrl+R**.	That's the shortcut for Fill Right. Filling right and filling down are very common, so it's good to remember and use their shortcuts.
4. Copy the total formula down column N.	
a) Select N8:N13.	
b) Press **Ctrl+D**.	The shortcut for Fill Down. You might notice that when you filled the formula down, Excel got rid of the border above N13. The fill process copies formulas and formatting, so there are sometimes side effects.
5. Use Auto Fill to enter the month column labels.	
a) Select B7.	
b) Point to the fill handle for the selection.	In the lower-right corner. The pointer takes the shape of a plus sign.
c) Drag to the right to extend the series all the way to **Dec**.	As you drag, Excel shows the last series value in a tip box.

92   Excel 2016 Level 1

Do This	How & Why
6. Click the **Auto Fill Options** button.	It is next to the last cell in the filled range. Depending on how Excel handled the fill, you see various options here. In this case, you can fill this as a simple copy (so all cells show "Jan"), as a series (which you did), and with or without formatting.
7. Save the workbook as `My Data Entry`.	
8. Activate the Series worksheet.	Click its tab. This worksheet contains some labels you'll use to experiment with the way the Fill options handle series.
9. Fill the Qtr1 label down to row 14.	Select A3, then drag its fill handle to A14. Excel recognizes that "Qtr" means "quarter," so it restarts numbering after "4."
10. Fill the Year 1 label down to row 14.	Excel just keeps adding to the year number.
11. Fill the 2016 label down to row 14.	In this case, Excel sees a single number and simply copies it down. To make a series of numbers, you often need to give Excel the first two values. But there is a quicker way.
12. Change the fill of the years to be a series.	
a) Click the AutoFill Options button.	To display options for how Excel is filling the range.
b) Click **Fill Series**.	To change the fill to be a series. Now the years go from 2016 to 2027.
13. Save the workbook.	

The completed budget in My Data Entry

Expense	Jan	Feb	Mar	Apr	May	Jun	Jul	Aug	Sep	Oct	Nov	Dec	Total
Rent	2000	2000	2000	2000	2000	2000	2000	2000	2000	2000	2000	2000	24000
Supplies	1000	1000	1000	1000	1000	1000	1000	1000	1000	1000	1000	1000	12000
Advertising	100	100	100	100	100	100	100	100	100	100	100	100	1200
Payroll	5000	5000	5000	5000	5000	5000	5000	5000	5000	5000	5000	5000	60000
Miscellaneous	800	800	800	800	800	800	800	800	800	800	800	800	9600
Totals:	8900	8900	8900	8900	8900	8900	8900	8900	8900	8900	8900	8900	106800

The complete series in My Data Entry

Qtr1	Year 1	2016
Qtr2	Year 2	2017
Qtr3	Year 3	2018
Qtr4	Year 4	2019
Qtr1	Year 5	2020
Qtr2	Year 6	2021
Qtr3	Year 7	2022
Qtr4	Year 8	2023
Qtr1	Year 9	2024
Qtr2	Year 10	2025
Qtr3	Year 11	2026
Qtr4	Year 12	2027

Replacing data

You can use the Replace command to search for particular data, and then to replace it with other data.

Exam Objective: MOS Excel Core 2.1.1

1. Click **Find & Select > Replace**.
    To display the Find and Replace window.
2. In the Find what box, enter the text for which you want to search.
3. In the Replace with box, enter the text with which you want to replace the found text.
4. Choose an option.
    - Click **Replace All** to replace all occurrences of the text.
    - Click **Replace** to replace the next occurrence.
    - Click **Find All** to display a list (in the window) of all the found text.
    - Click **Find** to find the next occurrence.
5. Click **Close**.

Exercise: Replacing a name with another name

My Data Entry is open.

Exam Objective: MOS Excel Core 2.1.1

Do This	How & Why
1. Activate the Find & Replace worksheet.	This worksheet contains invoice data. You want to reassign all of one sales rep's invoices to a different sales rep. There are 1000 rows of invoices, so this would be very tedious to do manually.
2. Click **Find & Select > Replace**.	The Find & Select button is on the Home tab, in the Editing group (on the far right). To display the Find and Replace window, with the Replace tab active.
3. In the Find what box, type `Hernandez`.	You will search for this sales rep, replacing the name with Lloyd where it is found.
4. In the Replace with box, type `Lloyd`.	
5. Click **Replace All**.	Excel displays a message saying there were 106 replacements. That would have been very slow to accomplish one at a time.
6. Click **OK**, then click **Close**.	To close the both the replacements message and the Find and Replace window.
7. Save and close the workbook.	

Excel 2016 Level 1

Assessment: Data entry shortcuts

You can use the Fill commands to extend series. True or false?

- True
- False

Auto Fill recognizes any series from a single value. True or false?

- True
- False

What could you do if you used Auto Fill and Excel copied instead of creating a series? Choose all that apply.

- Enter the series manually.
- Use the Fill, Series command.
- Try entering the first two values in the series before using Auto Fill.
- Try the Auto Fill Options button.

You can only replace found text one item at a time. True or false?

- True
- False

Module B: Paste options

When you copy and paste, Excel pastes all parts of what you copied: the contents of the cell (as a formula, if it's a formula), along with any formatting that had been applied to the copied cell. This is often useful, but sometimes you'll want just the values and not the formula (for a report, for example). Or you might get some formatting just the way you want it on one range, and then want to copy the same formatting, but not the contents, to another range.

Excel offers paste options that let you do those things and more.

You will learn how to:

- Copy formatting using the Format Painter
- Use paste options to paste values, formatting, formulas, or combinations
- Paste links to cells and ranges

Painting formats

You can use the Format Painter to copy the formatting from a selected cell or range and then paste it to another range. You can paste a copied format once, or many times, depending on how you use the tool.

Exam Objective: MOS Excel Core 2.2.3

1. Select the cell or range from which you want to copy the formatting.
2. Click or double-click **Format Painter**.
   The mouse pointer looks like this.

   - Click the tool to paste the copied formatting to a single location.
   - Double-click the tool to be able to paste the formatting to multiple locations.
3. Select the cell or range to which you want to copy the formatting.
4. Click any other cells or ranges to which you want to copy the formatting.
   Only if you double-clicked the tool. When you're done, press **Esc** to turn off the Format Painter.

Exercise: Painting a format from one range onto another

In this exercise, you'll quickly format a budget worksheet by using Format Painter to copy formats from one location to another.

Exam Objective: MOS Excel Core 2.2.3

Do This	How & Why
1. Open Pasting Options.	From the Manipulating Data folder. The first worksheet contains a café operating budget for year 1.
2. Select A8.	It is formatted as bold and centered. You'd like to use that formatting for all the column headings.
3. Click **Format Painter**.	In the ribbon's Clipboard group. The mouse pointer takes the shape of a cross and a paint brush, which allows you to drag over a cell or range to paste the copied formatting of the selected cell or range.
4. Select B8:N8.	The formatting is copied to the range. Also, the pointer returns to the default shape, meaning you can no longer paste the formatting.
5. Paste the format in N9 to the Totals row and column.	
a) Select N9.	
b) Double-click **Format Painter**.	When you double-click the tool, you can then paste to multiple ranges.
c) Select N10:N16.	To paste the formatting. Note that the Format Painter pointer is still active.
d) Select B17:N17.	You could continue to copy the formatting to many ranges.
e) Press **Esc**.	The tool is no longer active.
6. Place a bottom border below N16.	Select the cell, and click the bottom border button. The border was removed, because when you pasted the formatting from N9, its border (none) came along with the currency format. Pasting formats occasionally has unwanted side effects.
7. Activate the Year 2 worksheet.	It contains a year 2 budget but hasn't been formatted.
8. Copy the formatting from the year 1 budget to the year 2 budget.	
a) On the Year 1 worksheet, select A8:N17.	
b) Click **Format Painter**.	

Do This	How & Why
c) On the Year 2 worksheet, select A8.	When you paste formatting from a range, you need to select only the upper-left cell or the destination range. The entire budget is formatted the same as the year 1 budget.
9. Save the workbook as `My Pasting Options`.	

The Year 2 worksheet with pasted formatting

Sample Café Opening Budget													
Year 2													
Expense	Jan	Feb	Mar	Apr	May	Jun	Jul	Aug	Sep	Oct	Nov	Dec	Year Total
Rent	2200	2200	2200	2200	2200	2200	2200	2200	2200	2200	2200	2200	$ 26,400
Remodeling	2000	0	0	0	0	0	1000	0	0	0	0	0	$ 3,000
Legal	0	0	0	0	0	0	500		0	0	0	0	$ 500
Equipment	1000	0	0	0	0	0	0	0	0	0	0	0	$ 1,000
Supplies	1200	1200	1200	1200	1200	1200	1200	1200	1200	1200	1200	1200	$ 14,400
Advertising	100	100	100	100	100	100	100	100	100	100	100	100	$ 1,200
Payroll	6000	6000	6000	6000	6000	6000	6000	6000	6000	6000	6000	6000	$ 72,000
Miscellaneous	800	800	800	800	800	800	800	800	800	800	800	800	$ 9,600
Totals:	$ 13,300	$ 10,300	$ 10,300	$ 10,300	$ 10,300	$ 10,300	$ 11,800	$ 10,300	$ 10,300	$ 10,300	$ 10,300	$ 10,300	$128,100

Using paste options

After you copy data, you can choose to paste only the formatting, values, or formulas by using the Paste Options button. You can also paste various combinations of these.

Paste options

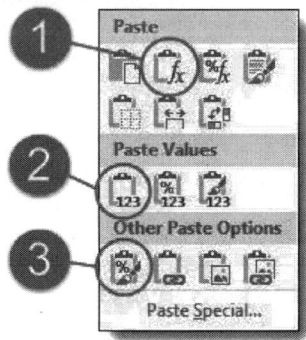

① *Paste Formulas* pastes all formulas from the copied cell or range, but not the formatting.

② *Paste Values* pastes only the resultant values of the copied formulas, not the formulas themselves or their formatting. This is very useful for reporting or for creating a snapshot of data at a particular point in time.

③ *Paste Formatting* pastes only the formatting of the copied cell or range, and not the formulas or values.

1. Copy the source cell or range.
2. Select the destination cell or range.
3. Select a paste option.
   - Paste, and then click the **Paste Options** button that appears next to the pasted data.
   - Click the Paste dropdown arrow on the ribbon (in the Clipboard group). When you use this method, you can hover over each option to preview how it will look when you click it.

Exercise: Pasting only formats or values

My Pasting Options is open.

Do This	How & Why
1. Observe the Year 3 worksheet.	It contains a year 3 budget, with slightly different figures from the other years. The total in N17 is 152500.
2. On the Year 2 worksheet, copy A8:N17.	
3. Observe how various paste options would work on the year 3 budget.	
a) On the Year 3 worksheet, select A8.	
b) Click the Paste dropdown arrow.	It's the arrow below the button on the ribbon. There are many ways to paste data.

Module B: Paste options

Do This	How & Why
c) Hover over [fx icon].	To see a preview of the effect the Paste Formulas button would have. It replaces all the data, but applies no formatting. We had the data we wanted, so this isn't a good option.
d) Hover over other buttons and observe their previews.	You can paste formulas, values, formatting, or combinations of these. All can be useful.
e) Click [% icon].	The Formatting button pastes only the formatting from the copied range, working like the Format Painter. The values and formulas in the destination are preserved (the total is still 152500).
4. Update the workbook.	
5. Observe the 3-Year Summary worksheet.	This will be a consolidated look at the three-year budget.
6. On the Year 1 worksheet, copy N9:N16.	You'll paste this data on the summary worksheet.
7. Paste the data on the 3-Year Summary worksheet.	
a) On 3-Year Summary, select B9.	
b) Paste the data.	The paste results in errors, because the formulas refer to cells that don't exist on this worksheet.
8. Paste only the values.	
a) Click the **Paste Options** button.	
b) Click [123 icon].	The Paste Values button pastes only the values—nice for creating a snapshot for a report like this.
9. Save the workbook.	

Excel 2016 Level 1   101

Pasting links

A link is really just a reference to another location. In a sense, every cell or range reference in every formula is a link. But you can refer to cells on other worksheets or workbooks, and those references are a bit more complex, because they have to include the name of the workbook, worksheet, or both. By pasting a link, you can avoid having to get that reference syntax right yourself.

1. Copy the cell or range to which you want to create a link.
2. Select the cell or range where you want to paste the link.
3. Display the paste options, and click [icon].
   This creates links to the copied cells in the destination range.

Exercise: Pasting links to data on another worksheet

My Pasting Options is open.

Do This	How & Why
1. Paste links to the first year's totals in the summary worksheet. a) On Year 1, copy N9:N16. b) On 3-Year Summary, select B9. c) In the paste options, click [icon]. d) Observe the pasted formula in B9.	 You will paste links on top of the values you pasted in the earlier exercise. The link is a reference to cell N9 on the Year 1 worksheet. 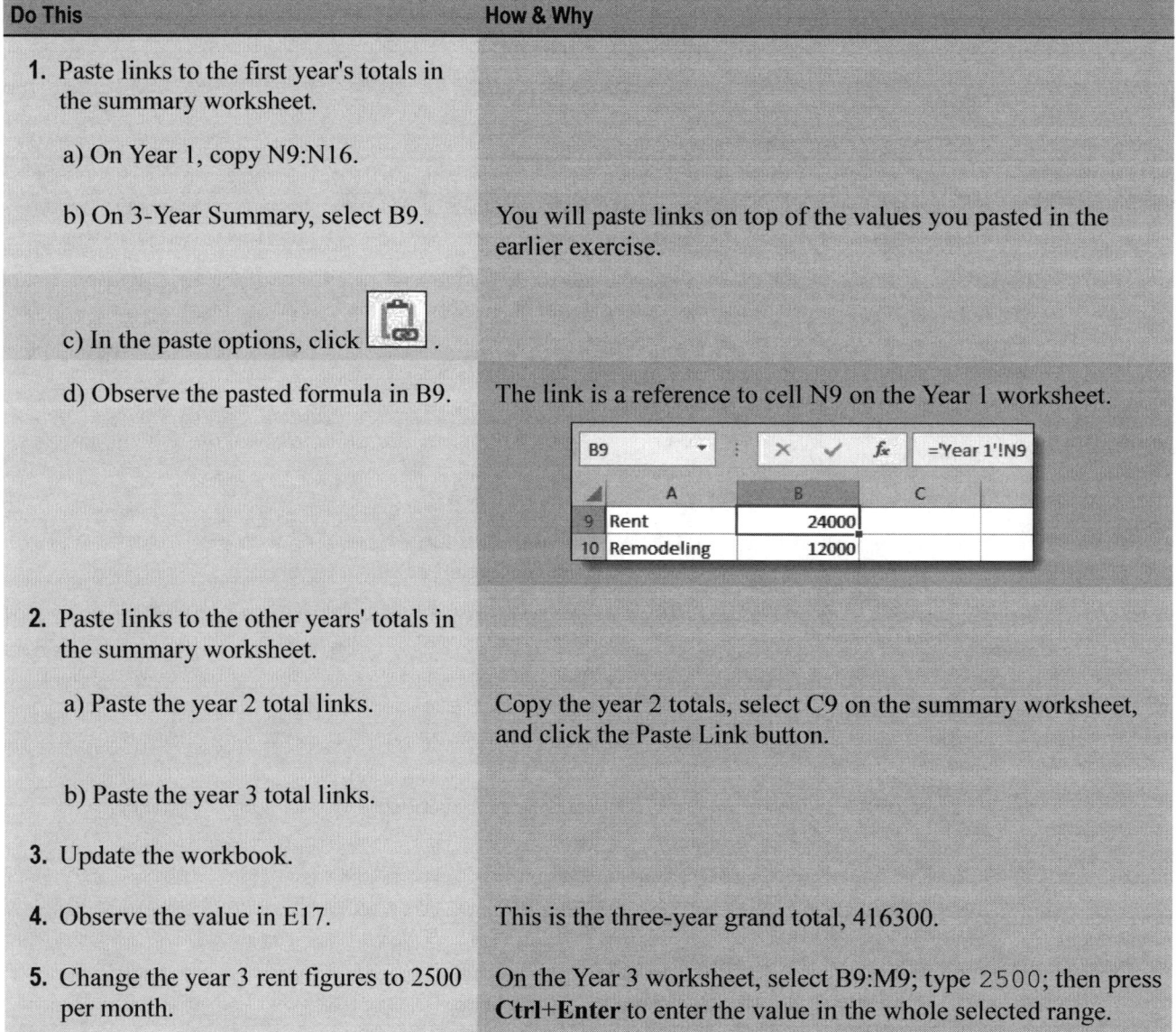
2. Paste links to the other years' totals in the summary worksheet. a) Paste the year 2 total links. b) Paste the year 3 total links.	 Copy the year 2 totals, select C9 on the summary worksheet, and click the Paste Link button.
3. Update the workbook.	
4. Observe the value in E17.	This is the three-year grand total, 416300.
5. Change the year 3 rent figures to 2500 per month.	On the Year 3 worksheet, select B9:M9; type 2500; then press **Ctrl+Enter** to enter the value in the whole selected range.

Do This	How & Why
6. Observe the change to the total on the summary worksheet.	The total is now 418100. Because the yearly totals here are linked to the totals on the other worksheets, and because those totals are calculated from the monthly values, everything updates properly.
7. Save and close the workbook.	

Assessment: Paste options

You can copy only the formulas of a cell or range, and not the formats or values. True or false?

- True
- False

How do you use the Format Painter to copy formatting to more than one destination?

- Hold down Ctrl while clicking the Format Painter.
- Double-click the Format Painter.
- Hold down Shift while clicking the Format Painter.
- Hold down Alt while clicking the destination ranges.

When you paste values, Excel creates a link to the source data. True or false?

- True
- False

Which of the following are possible with linking? Choose all that apply.

- Linking within a worksheet.
- Linking between worksheets in the same workbook.
- Linking between worksheets in different workbooks.

Module C: Inserting, deleting, and hiding

You often find that the structure you initially set up on a worksheet needs to be modified. You might need to add new rows of data in the middle of a table, or a new category of information as a new column. You can easily insert or delete cells and ranges, or entire rows or columns.

You can also hide rows or columns so that their data remains in the workbook but isn't visible. This is useful when some of the data in a workbook is appropriate for some people to see but not others, or when you don't want people distracted by too much detail.

You will learn how to:

- Insert and delete rows and columns
- Insert and delete ranges
- Hide and unhide rows and columns

Inserting and deleting rows and columns

When you insert a row or a column, Excel makes space by moving everything else down or over to the right. Similarly, if you delete a row or column, Excel slides the rest of the worksheet up or to the left.

Exam Objective: MOS Excel Core 1.3.5

1. Select the row(s) or column(s) you want to delete, or where you want to insert.
2. Click the appropriate command. There are a couple of places to find them.
   - In the ribbon's Cells group, in the Insert and Delete menus.
   - In the context menu that you display by right-clicking the selection.

Be careful when inserting within a structure that contains formulas. If you insert inside a range to which a formula refers, the formula will update to include the expanded range. But if you insert on the edge of such a range, the formula won't update.

Inserting and deleting cells and ranges

When you insert or delete single cells or ranges, you are changing the structure of the worksheet and you need to specify how Excel should handle the change.

Exam Objective: MOS Excel Core 2.1.5

1. Select the cell or range to be deleted, or where you want to insert.
2. Click the appropriate command.
   - If you use the ribbon's Delete or Insert menu, you can specify whether to insert and delete only cells, or entire rows and columns.
   - If you use the context menu, or click **Delete Cells** or **Insert Cells** on the ribbon, you'll need to specify what happens next.
3. If necessary, specify how to shift cells. The options are different for deleting and inserting.
   - Deleting options: **Shift cells left**, **Shift cells up**, **Entire row**, or **Entire column**.
   - Inserting options: **Shift cells right**, **Shift cells down**, **Entire row**, or **Entire column**.
4. Click **OK**.

Exercise: Inserting and deleting rows, columns, and ranges

Exam Objective: MOS Excel Core 1.3.5, 2.1.5

Do This	How & Why
1. Open Inserting Deleting Hiding.	From the Manipulating Data folder. This worksheet contains sales information. You're going to insert a new sales representative and a new product.
2. Insert a new row above row 16. a) Select row 16. b) Display the **Insert** menu, then click **Insert Sheet Rows**.	In the ribbon's Cells group, click the arrow below the Insert button to display the menu. There is now a blank row.
3. Copy the new Rep info into the blank row. a) On the Extra Data worksheet, copy A19:G19. b) Paste the copied data into the blank row on the Sales by Rep sheet. c) In the paste options, click .	Only the formulas are pasted, and the formatting matches the destination.
4. Insert space for a new product. a) Select D7:D18. Continued...	You'll insert the new product to the left of the Vela Herbal data.

Chapter 4: Manipulating data

Do This	How & Why
b) Right-click the selection, then click **Insert**.	To display the Insert window. You now need to choose where to shift the cells, or to shift entire rows or columns. In this case, shifting right or shifting the entire column works. But think about it carefully each time you perform this action, to avoid strange results. 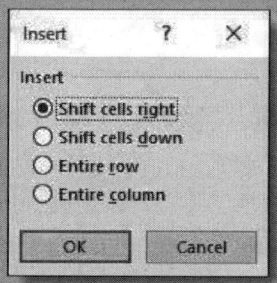
c) Click **OK**.	There is a blank space, and the rest of the data shifts right. You might need to adjust a column widths to fit data.
5. Copy the Phoenix Roast information into the blank space.	On the Extra Data worksheet, copy A5:A16, then paste it into the blank space on the Sales by Rep worksheet, pasting only formulas.
6. Delete Patterson's data.	
a) Select row 14.	
b) Right-click the selection, then click **Delete**.	When you select an entire row or column and then insert or delete, Excel just moves the rest of the worksheet up or down (for a row) or left or right (for a column) automatically. The row is gone, and the rest of the data has moved up.
7. Save the workbook as `My Inserting Deleting Hiding`.	

The Sales by Rep data after inserting and deleting

	A	B	C	D	E	F	G	H
7	Rep	Tucana Roast	Indus Tea	Phoenix Roast	Vela Herbal	Total	Comm Rt	Comm
8	Blackwell	$ 275.40	$ 680.40	$ 939.60	$ 1,150.20	$ 3,045.60	4%	$ 121.82
9	Daniels	$ 1,595.70	$ 2,914.20	$ 2,163.60	$ 2,533.50	$ 9,207.00	3%	$ 276.21
10	Franklin	$ 3,938.40	$ 2,623.50	$ 2,770.20	$ 3,206.70	$ 12,538.80	3%	$ 376.16
11	Hernandez	$ 3,324.60	$ 2,852.10	$ 3,851.10	$ 5,571.90	$ 15,599.70	3%	$ 467.99
12	Lloyd	$ 5,071.50	$ 6,271.20	$ 5,890.50	$ 6,158.70	$ 23,391.90	3%	$ 701.76
13	McCanney	$ 3,618.00	$ 4,826.70	$ 4,645.80	$ 6,976.80	$ 20,067.30	4%	$ 802.69
14	Sanchez	$ 4,054.50	$ 2,261.70	$ 3,958.20	$ 2,630.70	$ 12,905.10	4%	$ 516.20
15	Schiller	$ 4,765.50	$ 4,755.60	$ 4,764.60	$ 4,954.50	$ 19,240.20	4%	$ 769.61
16	Westlein	$ 4,488.30	$ 4,164.30	$ 3,832.20	$ 4,361.40	$ 16,846.20	3%	$ 505.39
17	Total:	$ 31,131.90	$ 31,349.70	$ 32,815.80	$ 37,544.40	$132,841.80		$ 4,537.84

Hiding rows and columns

You can hide rows or columns when you don't want them to distract people, or when they contain sensitive data.

Exam Objective: MOS Excel Core 1.4.2

1. Select the rows or columns that you want to hide.
2. Right-click the selection, and click **Hide**.
   You can also use the ribbon's Format Cells menu, but it takes a couple more clicks.

The selected rows or columns are no longer visible but are still in the workbook. You see a gap in the row numbers or column letters, with a small indicator between the headings.

Unhiding rows and columns

There are a couple of ways to display a hidden row or column.

- Select the rows or columns surrounding the hidden rows or columns, then, from In the context menu, click **Unhide**.
   Display the context menu by right-clicking the selection.
- Double-click the hidden row indicator between the headings.

Exercise: Hiding and unhiding sensitive information

My Inserting Deleting Hiding is open.

Exam Objective: MOS Excel Core 1.4.2

Do This	How & Why
1. Hide McCanney's data. a) Select row 13. b) Right-click, then click **Hide**. c) Observe the row headings.	 Row 13 is hidden, so the headings skip from 12 to 14. There is also a small indicator between the headings that shows there is a hidden row.
2. Hide the commission information. a) Select columns G:H. b) Right-click, then click **Hide**.	 The columns are hidden.
3. Unhide McCanney's data. a) Observe the hidden row indicator between the headings for rows 12 and 14. b) Double-click the hidden row indicator.	 To display the hidden row.
4. Save and then close the workbook.	

Sales by Rep with hidden columns (G:H)

	A	B	C	D	E	F
7	Rep	Tucana Roast	Indus Tea	Phoenix Roast	Vela Herbal	Total
8	Blackwell	$ 275.40	$ 680.40	$ 939.60	$ 1,150.20	$ 3,045.60
9	Daniels	$ 1,595.70	$ 2,914.20	$ 2,163.60	$ 2,533.50	$ 9,207.00
10	Franklin	$ 3,938.40	$ 2,623.50	$ 2,770.20	$ 3,206.70	$ 12,538.80
11	Hernandez	$ 3,324.60	$ 2,852.10	$ 3,851.10	$ 5,571.90	$ 15,599.70
12	Lloyd	$ 5,071.50	$ 6,271.20	$ 5,890.50	$ 6,158.70	$ 23,391.90
13	McCanney	$ 3,618.00	$ 4,826.70	$ 4,645.80	$ 6,976.80	$ 20,067.30
14	Sanchez	$ 4,054.50	$ 2,261.70	$ 3,958.20	$ 2,630.70	$ 12,905.10
15	Schiller	$ 4,765.50	$ 4,755.60	$ 4,764.60	$ 4,954.50	$ 19,240.20
16	Westlein	$ 4,488.30	$ 4,164.30	$ 3,832.20	$ 4,361.40	$ 16,846.20
17	Total:	$ 31,131.90	$ 31,349.70	$ 32,815.80	$ 37,544.40	$132,841.80

Assessment: Inserting, deleting, and hiding

When inserting or deleting, you do not always need to specify how to shift cells. True or false?

- True
- False

When you insert in a range referred to by a formula, under which circumstances does Excel automatically update the formula?

- When you insert within the endpoints of the reference, but not at the edge of the reference.
- When you insert at the edge of the reference, but not within the endpoints of the reference.
- Both when you insert within the endpoints of a reference and when you insert at the edge of a reference.

When you hide a row or column, its data is removed from the workbook. True or false?

- True
- False

Summary: Manipulating data

You should now know:

- How to use Fill commands to copy data to adjacent cells, and how to use Auto Fill to copy data or extend series
- About paste options, and how to paste only values, formulas, formats, or combinations of those parts of cell data
- How to insert and delete rows and columns, about the difference when you insert or delete cells and ranges, and how to hide and unhide rows and columns

Synthesis: Manipulating data

In this synthesis exercise, you'll work with customer sales data to experiment with data entry shortcuts, paste options, inserting of data, and hiding of information.

1. Open Manipulating Data Synthesis from the Manipulating Data folder.
   This workbook contains customer sales information.
2. Paint the format from A8 onto the rest of the column headings.
3. In F9, enter the correct formula for the discounted total sales. (Hint: multiply the pre-discount amount by 1 minus the discount percentage.)
4. Use **Fill Down** to copy the formula to the rest of column F.
5. Use Auto Fill and the paste options to copy the formatting from row 9 to the rest of the data.
6. Insert a blank row above the Phlogistix data (row 34).
7. Copy only the formulas for the Opera Bohemia data on the Extra Data worksheet into the blank space.
8. Hide the Discount and Pre-Discount data.
9. Save the workbook as **My Manipulating Data Synthesis**, then close it.

The completed My Manipulating Data Synthesis workbook

	A	B	C	F	G
8	Customer	Rep	Region	Total Sales	Notes
9	Accounts Now	McCanney	International	$ 3,924.45	Send invoices by mail only; contact to renegotiate discount rate.
10	Award Sportswear	Westlein	US	$ 2,258.28	
11	Blastera	Westlein	US	$ 3,227.04	Contact to renegotiate discount rate.
12	BlazerFire	Daniels	US	$ 1,689.66	
13	Brocadero	Westlein	US	$ 2,034.72	Send invoices by mail only.

Chapter 5: Charts

You will learn how to:

- Create simple charts
- Change a chart's type and add elements to it

Module A: Creating charts

Charts are nothing more than a pictorial representation of your data. Sometimes, a picture really does say a thousand words or, more accurately, convey what a thousand numbers can't. Creating a simple chart requires little more than selecting data and clicking a button.

You will learn:

- How to create a simple line chart
- About the connection between a chart and its source data

About charts

An Excel *chart* shows you, in one of many ways, pictures of *series* of numbers. In a *pie chart*, for example, a series of numbers appears as slices of a pie that represents a whole.

A pie chart

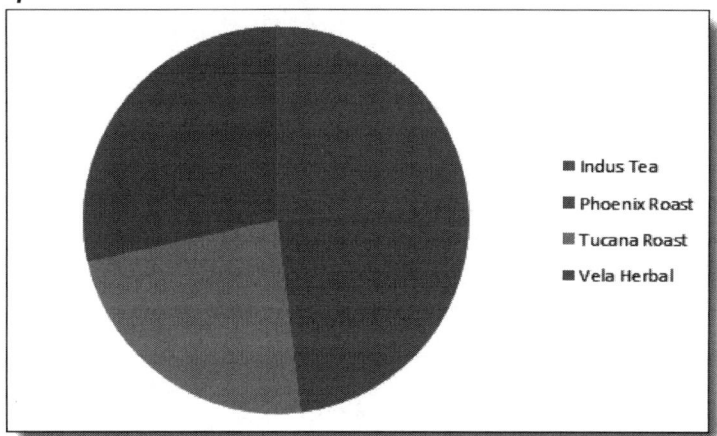

In a *line chart*, on the other hand, each series is a line, with points representing each individual value.

A line chart

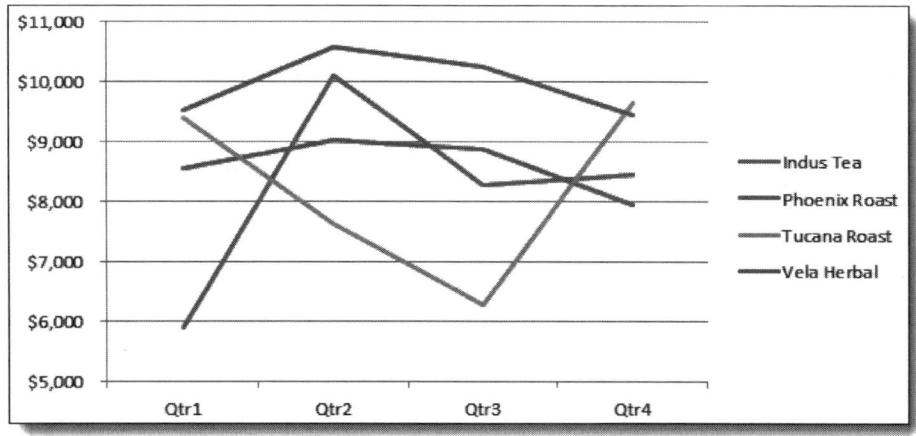

Excel makes it easy to create simple charts like these. But you also have the power to make complex charts that compare different kinds of data, overlay different chart types, and highlight the point you want to make.

Creating simple charts

 Exam Objective: MOS Excel Core 5.1.1

Creating a simple chart is quick and easy.

1. Select the data for which you want to create a chart.

   To get the most out of Excel's automation, be sure to select both the headings and the data. Don't select totals unless you definitely want them in the chart.

   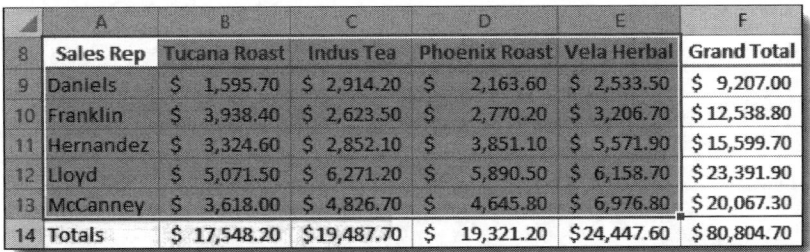

2. On the ribbon's Insert tab, in the Charts group, click a chart-type button.

   A gallery appears showing a selection of sub-types of the chart type you clicked.

   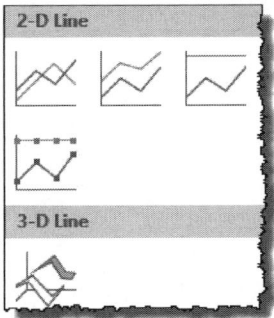

3. Click a chart sub-type.

   Excel creates a chart of the type you select right on the worksheet you are on.

When a chart is active, Excel adds two Chart Tools tabs to the ribbon. You can use these tabs to change and format the selected chart.

Moving and sizing charts

When you create a chart, Excel puts it on the worksheet with the data used to create it. But you can move a chart within that worksheet, to a different worksheet, or to its own chart sheet.

Exam Objective: MOS Excel Core 5.2.1, 5.2.4

- To move a chart within a worksheet, point to its edge and drag it.
- To move a chart to another worksheet or its own sheet, go to the Chart Tools Design tab, and click **Move Chart**.
  - To move the chart to its own chart sheet, click **New Sheet**, enter a name, and click **OK**.
  - To move the chart to a different worksheet, click **Object in**, select a worksheet, and click **OK**.

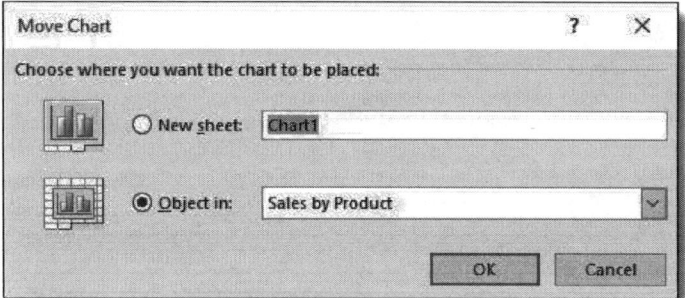

- To resize a chart, click it to select it, then draft one of its sizing handles.

Chart source data

Charts are linked to the data from which they're created. Because of this, any time you change that source data, the chart changes as well, reflecting the new data. As you make changes, the chart will move, or animate, to show the change.

Exercise: Creating a simple line chart

Exam Objective: MOS Excel Core 5.1.1, 5.2.1, 5.2.4

Do This	How & Why
1. Open Creating Charts.	From the Charts data folder. The worksheet contains monthly sales figures for five sales representatives ("reps"). You'll create a line chart for this data.
2. Create a line chart from the data.	
a) Select A8:M13.	Note that you are selecting the labels (months and rep names) as well as the monthly sales figures. You are not selecting the totals. You might use totals in a different chart, but not in this one.
b) On the ribbon, click the **Insert** tab.	The Insert tab provides commands for inserting shapes, objects, charts, and more.
c) In the Charts group, click [icon].	The Line Chart button. A gallery of line-chart types appears.

Do This	How & Why
d) Click the first 2D line-chart button.	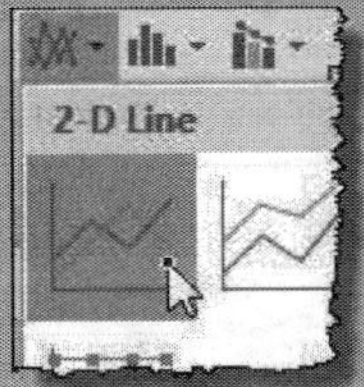 To create a line chart in the current worksheet.
3. Move the chart below the data.	
a) Point to the edge of the chart.	The pointer becomes a four-headed arrow.
b) Drag the chart below the data.	
4. Widen the chart.	
a) Point to the sizing handle on the right edge of the chart.	The pointer takes the shape of a two-headed arrow. 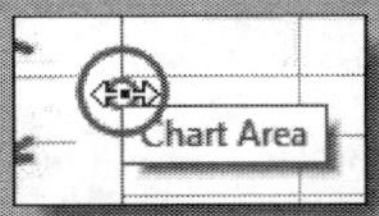
b) Drag to the right to increase the size of the chart.	
5. Observe McCanney's July figure on the chart.	It is quite high, above $3,500.
6. In H13, enter `2500`.	The figure changes, and so does the chart, because the lines and data are linked.
7. In the chart, click McCanney's line.	Notice the formula on the Formula bar. That SERIES function defines the series of data that becomes that line. You don't actually need to work directly with these functions, but they're the reason the data link works.
8. Save the workbook as `My Creating Charts`.	
9. Move the chart to its own chart sheet.	
a) Select the chart.	Click it. It might already be selected. Notice that, when a chart is selected, a new group of Chart Tools tabs appears on the ribbon.
b) Click the Design tab.	The Chart Tools, Design ribbon tab appears.
c) Click **Move Chart**.	The Move Chart window appears.
d) Select **New sheet**, type `My Line Chart`, and click **OK**.	
10. Update and close the workbook.	An example follows.

The My Line Chart chart sheet

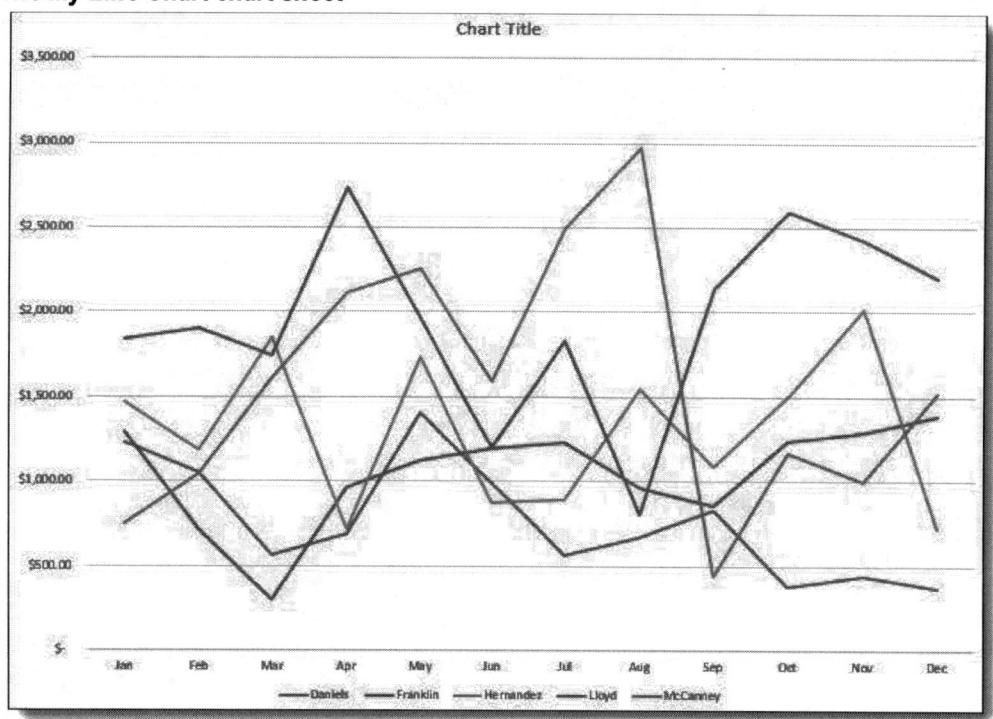

Assessment: Creating charts

You should not select labels when selecting data for a chart. True or false?

- True
- False

How do you update a chart after changing its source data?

- By press F9.
- By clicking the Update button on the Design tab of the ribbon.
- You don't need to do anything, because the chart will update automatically.

Which of the following are ways to move a chart? Choose all that apply.

- By selecting the chart and using the arrow keys.
- By dragging.
- By clicking the Move Chart button.

Module B: Chart types and elements

Charts can be of various types, such as line, bar, and pie. They can have many elements, including legends, axes, grids, titles, and labels.

You will learn how to:

- Create a pie chart
- Control style and layout in a chart
- Create a column chart
- Switch the plotting of rows and columns in a chart
- Control and format chart elements

Chart types

Excel has many chart types that you can use for various kinds of data, and to make various points to an audience. Within each type, there are also many sub-types.

- *Column charts* show data as columns, either single columns for each value, or stacked to show how individual values relate to totals for a particular category. They are useful for showing magnitude in an obvious way.
- *Line charts* show series of values as points along a line. They are great for showing trends.
- *Pie charts* show how values relate to a whole. The data you select for a pie chart should have only one series of values.
- *Bar charts* are really the same as column charts, with the bars running horizontally (as opposed to columns, which run vertically).
- *Area charts* combine line charts and columns by filling in the areas below the lines.
- *Scatter charts* show coordinates, and are useful for looking at how two related variables are distributed.

Excel has many other chart types as well that are useful for other types of data. If you're not sure what type of chart to use, try clicking the **Recommended Charts** button to see what Excel suggests.

Changing chart type

After you set the type of a chart, you can very easily change its layout and style.

  Exam Objective: MOS Excel Core 5.2.3

1. Select the chart.
2. On the Chart Tools, Design tab, click **Change Chart Type**.
   To display the Change Chart Type window.

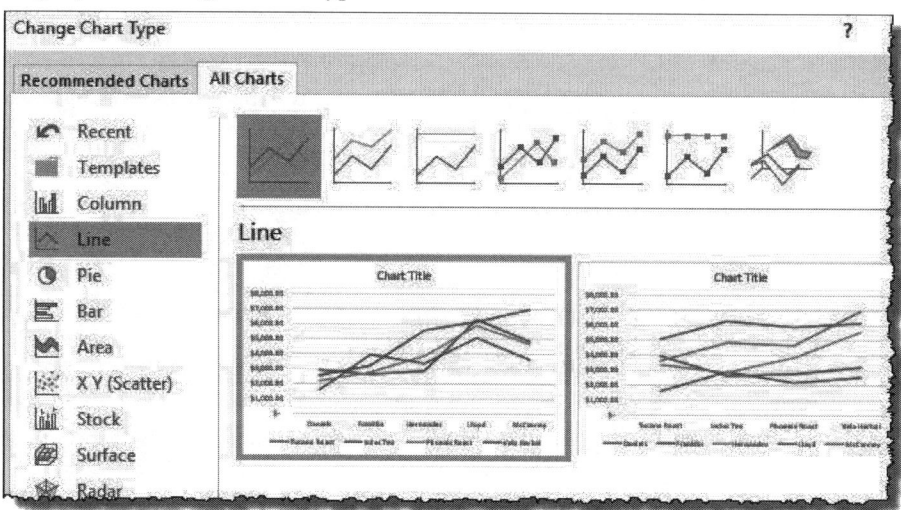

3. Select a type on the left, then a sub-type, and click **OK**.
   You can get a preview of what your data will look like in a particular chart type by hovering over it.

The chart type changes, and now the Chart Tools, Design tab gives you many options for layout and style that are specific to the new type. Simply click Quick Layout and choose an option, or select a style to see what it will look like.

Exercise: Creating a pie chart and changing style and layout

  Exam Objective: MOS Excel Core 5.2.3

Do This	How & Why
1. Open **Chart Types and Elements**.	From the Charts data folder.
2. Create a pie chart of the sales reps' grand totals. a) Select A8:A13, then hold down **Ctrl**, and select F8:F13.	Remember, you can hold down the Ctrl key to select multiple ranges. When you create a pie chart, you want to select only the labels and a single series of values. |	A	B	C	D	E	F
---	---	---	---	---	---	---
8	Sales Rep	Tucana Roast	Indus Tea	Phoenix Roast	Vela Herbal	Grand Total
9	Daniels	$ 1,595.70	$ 2,914.20	$ 2,163.60	$ 2,533.50	$ 9,207.00
10	Franklin	$ 3,938.40	$ 2,623.50	$ 2,770.20	$ 3,206.70	$12,538.80
11	Hernandez	$ 3,324.60	$ 2,852.10	$ 3,851.10	$ 5,571.90	$15,599.70
12	Lloyd	$ 5,071.50	$ 6,271.20	$ 5,890.50	$ 6,158.70	$23,391.90
13	McCanney	$ 3,618.00	$ 4,826.70	$ 4,645.80	$ 6,976.80	$20,067.30
14	Totals	$ 17,548.20	$19,487.70	$ 19,321.20	$24,447.60	$80,804.70	

Do This	How & Why
b) On the Insert tab, click  .	The Pie Chart gallery appears.
c) Select the first sub-type.	The simple, 2D pie chart.
3. Try different styles.	On the Chart Tools, Design tab, hover over various chart style options. This changes the color scheme.
4. Choose the Quick Layout with percentages and labels	Click the **Quick Layout**, then click the layout you want. This is a very clear layout. But it might not be appropriate, with too many slices in the pie chart. 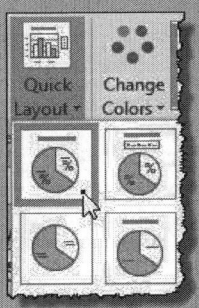
5. Save the workbook as `My Chart Types and Elements`.	

Switching rows and columns

When you create a chart, Excel makes assumptions about how you want to see the data. Usually, Excel is right, but sometimes, you want to see lines that map to your columns instead of your rows, or vice versa. To change this, simply select the chart, and click **Switch Row/Column** (on the Chart Tools, Design tab).

Exam Objective: MOS Excel Core 5.1.3

Exercise: Creating a column chart and switching rows and columns

My Chart Types and Elements is open.

Exam Objective: MOS Excel Core 5.1.3

In this exercise, you'll create a column chart, then change it to a stacked column chart, and finally switch rows and columns to see a column for each product, rather than one for each sales rep.

Do This	How & Why
1. Create a column chart for the product sales by sales rep.	
a) Select A8:E13.	This selects the data and the labels, but not the totals row or column.
b) Click [icon], then the first 3D sub-type.	The Insert Column Chart button is on the Insert tab. The chart is quite busy-looking with individual columns for every rep and product combination.
2. Change the type to a stacked, 3D column.	
a) Click **Change Chart Type**.	On the Chart Tools, Design tab.
b) Click the Stacked 3D Column tile.	[icon] To view options for plotting the data as this type of chart. You can plot the reps as the series, or the products.
c) Click **OK**.	This is a much clearer presentation of the data. There is one column for each sales rep, representing her total sales. Each bar is broken into parts for each product. But what if you wanted to see a bar for each product?

Do This	How & Why
3. Click **Switch Row/Column**.	This is a very useful feature for making your charts show what you really want them to show. 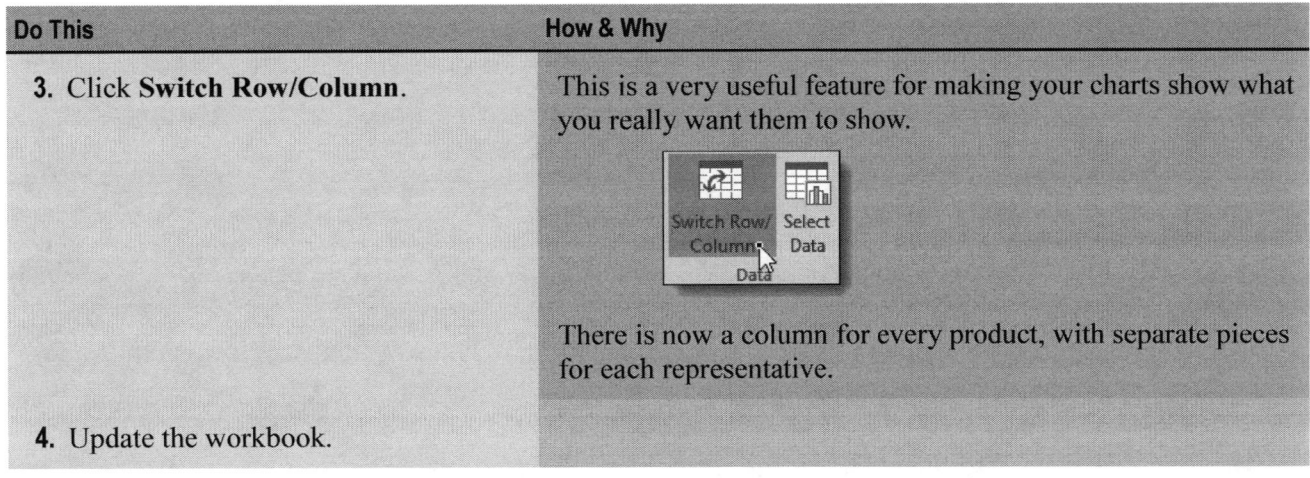 There is now a column for every product, with separate pieces for each representative.
4. Update the workbook.	

Chart elements

Charts come from the data you select when you make them. And each element of the chart represents either something in that data or something you can add to the chart and control.

Chart elements

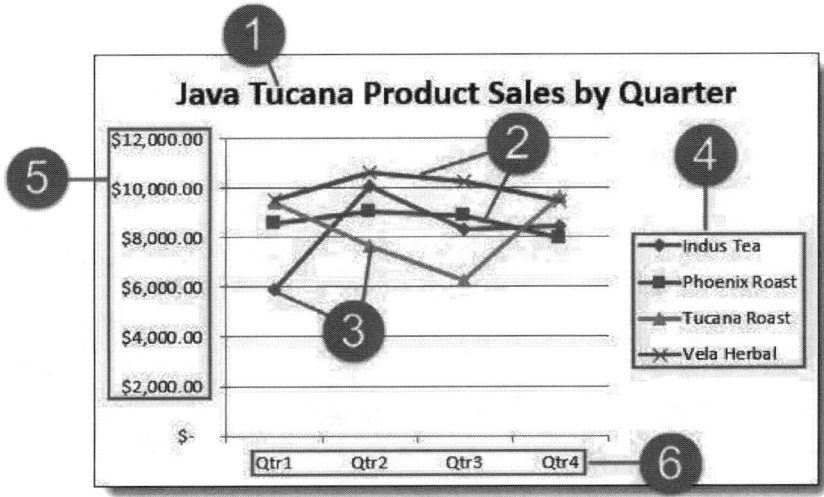

① The *chart title* is usually something you will add to the chart, rather than something that comes from the selected data.

② *Data series* are the series of values that show up in lines, columns, or other ways in your charts.

③ *Data points* represent the individual values within data series.

④ The *legend* identifies the data series in the chart.

⑤ The *value axis* shows the scale for what the chart is measuring. You can exercise enormous control over how the value axis appears and works. It is often plotted vertically, as in this example, but it does not have to be.

⑥ The *category axis* shows the categories of information within the data series. It is usually the horizontal axis, but not always.

Chapter 5: Charts

Controlling chart elements

How you control different chart elements depends to some extent on the element.

 Exam Objective: MOS Excel Core 5.2.2

- Activate the Chart Tools, Layout tab, click Add Chart Element, click the element you want to add, then select an option from the gallery.
- Select the element, and right-click it to display a context menu. This is often a quicker route to the same options.
- For labels, such as the title or an axis label, simply click the label, enter the text as you would like it to appear, and press **Enter**.

Controlling the value axis

Right-click the value axis, and click **Format Axis** to display the Format Axis window, which gives you many options for controlling the axis and the appearance of the chart in general.

 Exam Objective: MOS Excel Core 5.2.3

- *Axis Options* give you control over things like number format, minimum and maximum values, the scale of the chart, tick marks, display units, and more.
- *Text Options* let you format how the text appears next to the axis.

Exercise: Controlling the elements of a line chart

My Chart Types and Elements is open.

 Exam Objective: MOS Excel Core 5.2.2

Do This	How & Why
1. Activate the Product by Quarter worksheet.	It contains product sales data by quarter, and a simple line chart of that data.
2. Change the chart to **Layout 1**.	
a) Select the chart.	
b) Click **Quick Layout**, then the first layout option.	On the Chart Tools, Design tab. The chart now has a title and a value axis label.
3. Change the title to `Products by Quarter`.	
a) Click **Chart Title**.	To select it.
b) Type `Products by Quarter`, and press **Enter**.	
4. Click **Add Chart Element > Legend > Bottom**.	To move the legend below the chart.

Do This	How & Why
5. Change the value axis title to US Dollars.	Select **Axis Title**, type US Dollars, and press **Enter**.
6. Observe the lines.	Because the values mostly fall within a 4000-dollar range, it's a bit hard to see a lot of difference. You'll change the minimum value for the axis to increase the contrast of the scale.
7. Change the value axis minimum to 5000.	
a) Right-click the value axis, and click **Format Axis**.	The Format Axis pane appears.
b) Under Axis Options, In the Minimum box, type **5000**, then press **Enter**.	The change in the chart is immediate. Note the Reset button next to the Minimum box; this resets the axis to its original minimum value.
c) Click the Close button in the Format Axis pane.	Format Axis Axis Options ▼ Text Options The difference in the lines is much clearer with a higher minimum value on the axis.
8. Remove the decimal places on the value axis.	
a) Display the Format Axis pane for the value axis.	Right-click it, and click **Format Axis**.
b) Under Axis Options, near the bottom, click **Number**.	
c) Change the decimal places to 0.	
d) Close the Format Axis pane.	The axis looks much cleaner without the unnecessary decimal places.
9. Save and then close the workbook.	An example follows.

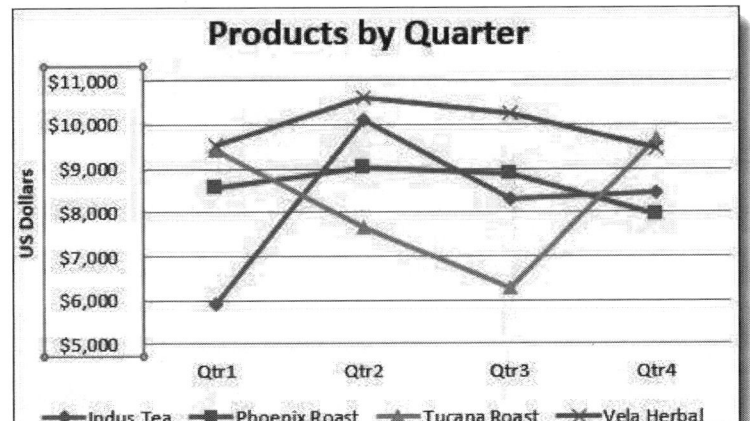

Assessment: Chart types and elements

You can specify the type for a chart only when you create the chart. True or false?

- True
- False

Which type of chart is best for showing trends?

- Pie
- Line
- Column
- Scatter

The only way to change the axis Excel uses for your data is to transpose the data in a worksheet and create a new chart. True or false?

- True
- False

Not all chart elements come from the data you select when you create the chart. True or false?

- True
- False

The only way to control the format of the value axis numbers by changing the format in the source data. True or false?

- True
- False

Summary: Charts

You should now know how to:

- Create a simple chart and move it either within a worksheet or to a chart sheet, and about the link between a chart and its source data
- Change a chart's type, layout, and style; create pie and stacked or unstacked column charts; switch rows and columns; control various chart elements including titles, the legend, and the value axis

Synthesis: Charts

In this exercise, you'll open a workbook with more sales data, and then create pie, column, and line charts from the data it contains. You'll also change chart elements and how the chart is plotted.

1. Open Charts Synthesis from the Charts data folder.
2. Create a 3D pie chart that shows sales by region.
3. Use a Quick Layout to show both labels and percentages on the pie chart.
4. Move the chart to the Charts worksheet.
5. Change the chart title to `Sales by Region`.
6. Save the workbook as `My Charts Synthesis`.
7. Create a stacked column chart of product sales by region, and move it to a separate chart sheet.
8. Switch rows and columns so the chart shows one column for each region. You might have to click on the chart to see the change.
9. Update the workbook.
10. From the data on the Regions by Month worksheet, create a 3D line chart.
11. Delete the text "Eurozone" from the right of the chart. (Select it, then delete it.) Sometimes, Excel will include something you don't want on a chart.
12. Add `Monthly Sales by Region` as a title.
13. Change the minimum for the value axis to `1700` and the maximum to `6100`.
14. Save and close the workbook.

The completed 3D line chart

Chapter 6: Output

You will learn how to:

- Split and arrange worksheet windows
- Print worksheets and control how they print by using print setup options
- Save workbooks to other formats and share workbooks with other users

Module A: Managing worksheet windows

You can use various techniques, such as splitting and arranging windows, to view worksheets and workbooks exactly the way you want to.

You will learn how to:

- Split worksheets and freeze panes to keep headings in view
- Manage and arrange multiple windows

Workbook windows

It's often useful to have more than one workbook open, so that you can compare information or move or copy it between workbooks. Sometimes, you want to arrange multiple workbooks so you can see more than one at a time. You also might want to see more than one part of a single workbook, or freeze part of it (such as headings) in place. Various View tab commands make all of this simple.

Splitting worksheets

 Exam Objective: MOS Excel Core 1.4.5

By splitting a worksheet, you can view two parts of it at the same time. This is especially useful for keeping headings in view while scrolling through a large worksheet. You can split a worksheet vertically, horizontally, or both.

- Select a row or column, and then, on the View tab, click **Split**.

    This places a split above the selected row or to the left of the selected column, cutting the window into two panes.

- Select a cell and then click **Split**.

    This places a split above and to the left of the selected cell, effectively cutting the worksheet window into four panes, each with its own scroll bars.

After you split a worksheet, you can remove the split by clicking **Split** again.

Freezing panes

After you split a worksheet, you can freeze the panes to lock them into place. This is great for keeping column or row headings in place as you scroll through large worksheets.

 Exam Objective: MOS Excel Core 1.4.5

1. Either split the worksheet as you want, or select where you want the frozen, split panes to be.
   - Select a single cell to split and freeze panes above and to the left of the selection.
   - Select a row to split and freeze panes above that row.
   - Select a column to split and freeze panes to the left of the column.
2. On the View tab, click **Freeze Panes**, and then click an option.

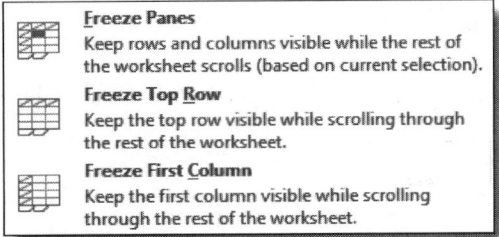

   - Click **Freeze Panes** to freeze at the current location.
   - Click **Freeze Top Row** or **Freeze First Column** to freeze the top row or the first column. Using this method, you do not need to first select a cell, row, or column.

After you freeze panes, you can unfreeze them by clicking **Freeze Panes**, then clicking **Unfreeze Panes**.

Exercise: Splitting a large worksheet

 Exam Objective: MOS Excel Core 1.4.5

Do This	How & Why
1. Open Worksheet Windows.	From the `Output` data folder.
2. Scroll to view the data.	The worksheet has hundreds of rows of data, and as you scroll, the headings disappear from view.
3. Split the window above row 10.	
a) Select row 10.	
b) On the View tab, click **Split**.	The button is in the Window group. The window splits into two panes, each with its own scroll bars, so you can scroll each separately.
4. Click **Freeze Panes**, then click **Freeze Panes**.	The separate scroll bars disappear, and the window looks like a single pane again.
5. Scroll down.	As you do, the rows above row 10 (row 9 is where the headings are) stay locked in place.
6. Click **Split**.	To remove the split. When a window is already split, the split button removes the split.
7. Freeze panes above row 10.	
a) Select row 10.	
b) Click **Freeze Panes**, then click **Freeze Panes**.	You can freeze panes directly in this manner without first splitting the window.
8. Click **Freeze Panes**.	When panes are frozen, the first command in the gallery is Unfreeze Panes.
9. Press **Esc**.	To close the Freeze Panes gallery.
10. Save the workbook as `My Worksheet Windows`.	

Multiple windows

You can open more than one window of the current workbook, or multiple workbooks with their own windows. When you have multiple windows, you can arrange them to see them arranged vertically, horizontally, tiled, or cascaded. Vertical and horizontal are self-explanatory. The figures show what tiled and cascaded windows look like.

Tiled windows

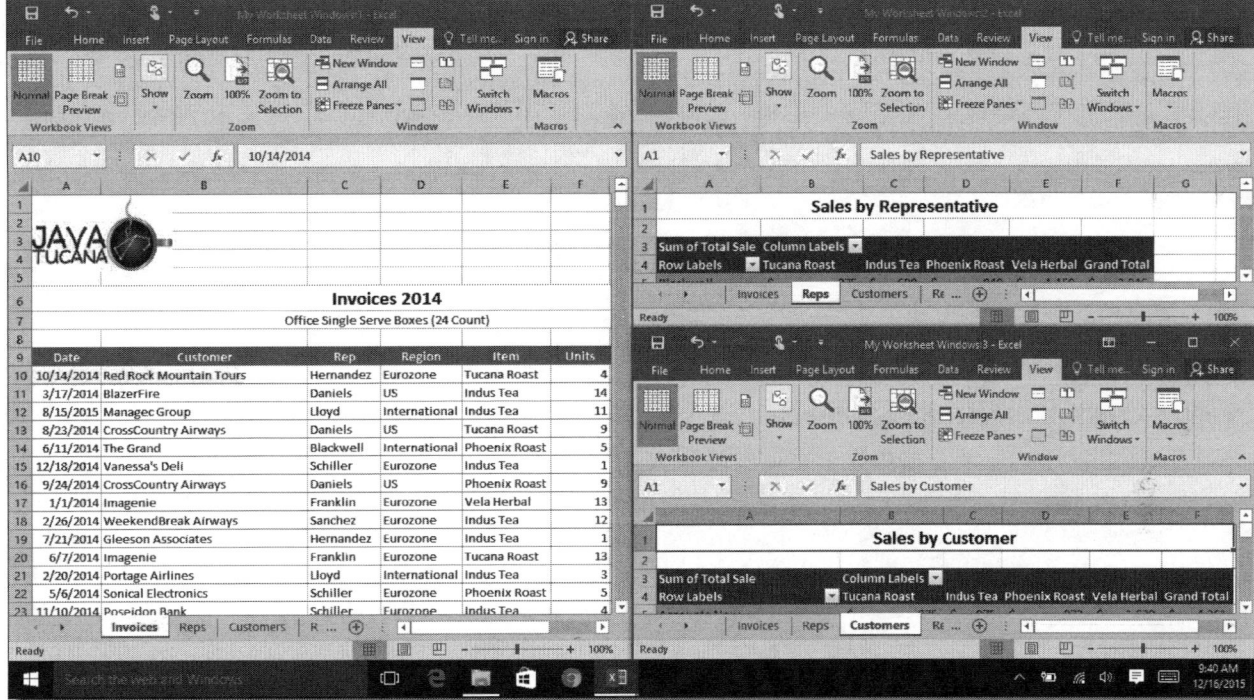

Cascaded windows

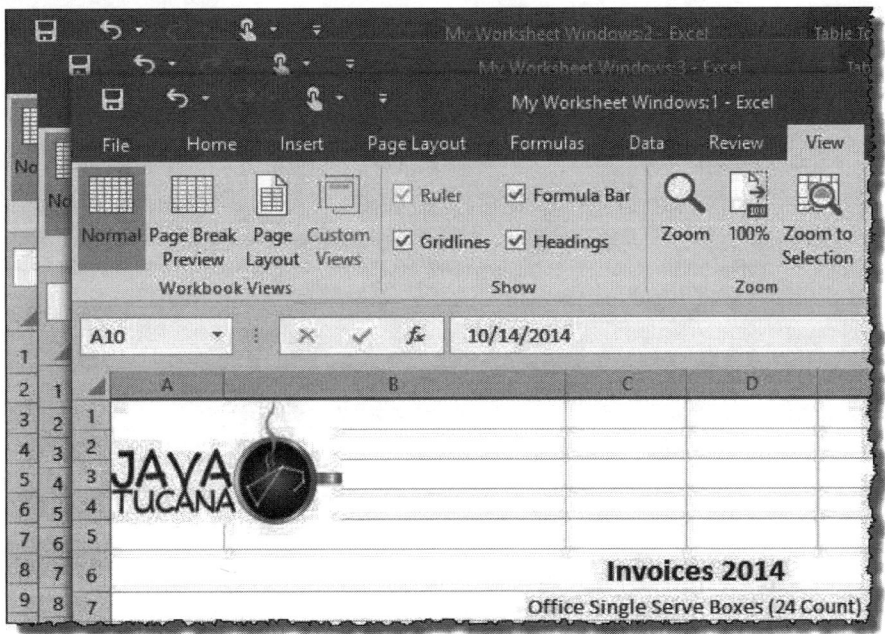

Opening new windows

You can open new windows for the current workbook. This can be useful when you want to view two parts of a worksheet at the same time, or when you want to view different worksheets within a workbook at the same time.

1. Activate the window for which you want to open a new window.
2. On the View tab, in the Window group, click **New Window**.

If you have the current window maximized in Excel, you don't see anything obvious within the Excel window. But there is be a new window icon on the Windows task bar. You can move among open windows by clicking **Switch Windows**, then clicking the name of the window you want to see.

Arranging windows

When you want to view multiple open windows at the same time, you can arrange them.

Exam Objective: MOS Excel Core 1.4.5

1. Open all the windows you want to arrange.
2. On the View tab, click Arrange All.

   The Arrange Windows window appears.

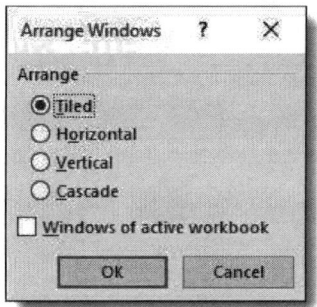

3. Check **Windows of the active workbook** to arrange only the open windows of the active workbook.
4. Click the arrangement you want.
   - *Tiled* arranges the windows in a grid.
   - *Horizontal* arranges the windows so each uses the full width of the Excel window, above and below each other.
   - *Vertical* arranges the windows side-by-side.
   - *Cascade* arranges the windows in a stack with their title bars visible, making it easy to move among them.
5. Click **OK**.

When you have multiple windows open for a workbook, you can close a window individually by using it's close button. If you close the workbook using the Close command in Backstage view (the File tab), however, Excel will close all the windows and will remember the window arrangement next time you open the workbook. This works something like the old Workspace command in Excel 2010 and before.

Exercise: Arranging all the worksheets in a workbook

My Worksheet Windows is open.

Exam Objective: MOS Excel Core 1.4.5

Do This	How & Why
1. Observe the worksheet tabs.	There are four worksheets in this workbook. We'd like to be able to see all of them at once.
2. On the View tab, click **New Window**.	Although you created a new window, it might not be immediately obvious.
3. On the taskbar, click [icon].	

This is the Excel taskbar icon. There are now two windows open for the current workbook.

4. Click **New Window** two more times.	To create two more windows for the workbook, a total of four.
5. On the View tab, click **Arrange All**.	To open the Arrange Windows window. Here, you can decide how you want to arrange the open windows. You will tile the windows of the current workbook. Tiled is the default choice.
6. Check **Windows of the active workbook**, then click **OK**.	You are now seeing the first worksheet in each of the four, tiled windows.
7. Activate the other three worksheets in their own windows.	
a) In the lower-left window, activate **Reps**.	
b) In the upper-right window, activate **Customers**.	
c) In the lower-right window, activate **Regions**.	
8. Save My Worksheet Windows.	Although you arranged the worksheets, that arrangement is not saved with the workbook.
9. Click **File**, then **Close** to close the workbook.	To close all the open windows of the current workbook. When you open the workbook, Excel will again open the number of windows that were open when you last saved it.

Assessment: Managing worksheet windows

The Split command always creates four window panes. True or false?

- True
- False

You do not have to split windows before freezing panes. True or False?

- True
- False

Module B: Printing worksheets

Although we live in a world in which it is very easy to share information electronically, you sometimes need to print your worksheets in order to share hard copies of them. Excel makes it very simple to print the active worksheet with a single click, but also gives you enormous control over how the worksheet prints: titles, headers and footers, scale, print area, gridlines, and more.

You will learn how to:

- Preview and print the active worksheet with current settings
- Print an entire workbook or selected worksheets
- Control print setup options, such as scale, orientation, gridlines, headings, and margins
- Control the print area and how to set print titles that appear on every page
- Create headers and footers

Printing

In order to print, you need a couple of things.

- Access to a printer, either by a local connection to your computer or through a network
- A printer driver for the printer you want to use

Generally, these things are set up for you at your workplace. After they are set up, printing a worksheet can be a simple matter of clicking one or two buttons. But you might find that a default printout doesn't give you what you want. It might be spread across pages strangely, or not include the headings you want where you want them. For this reason, you should preview your worksheets before you print them. Then you can make changes to the print settings before wasting paper.

Previewing a worksheet

In Backstage view, you can see a preview of how your worksheet will look when printed.

1. Click **File**, then click **Print**.
   To display the Print screen in Backstage view. Here, you can change print settings and see how they'll affect the printout.
2. Click the preview, and then use the Page Down and Page Up keys to move through the preview.
3. Make any changes to settings.
4. Click **Print** to print, or press **Esc** to return to the workbook.

Printing a worksheet

When the worksheet preview looks like you want it in Backstage view, simply click **Print** to print it.

Exercise: Previewing and printing a worksheet

Do This	How & Why
1. Open Printing Worksheets.	From the Output data folder. This workbook contains two sales report worksheets and a worksheet of invoice data from which the reports were generated. The current worksheet, Reps by Month, has data that is wide but not long.
2. Click **File**, then click **Print**.	To display the Print screen, which shows various settings for how the worksheet will print, as well as a preview of the first page of the printout.
3. Click the preview, then press **Page Down**.	To move to the second page of the printout. The pages break vertically, in the middle of the data. There are certainly better ways to present this.
4. Observe the Print button.	If you click it, the current worksheet will print on the current printer immediately, using all current settings. We're not going to do that now.
5. Press **Esc**.	To return to the workbook.
6. Activate the Customers by Item worksheet.	This worksheet has data that is narrow but relatively long.
7. Preview the worksheet.	Click **File**, then **Print**.
8. Click the preview, then press **Page Down**.	This worksheet would also print with two pages, breaking horizontally. It looks better than the other one, but there would be no headings on the second page.
9. Press **Esc**.	To return to the workbook. Notice that after previewing a worksheet, Excel displays dotted lines that show you where the page breaks will be when you print.

Print setup options

You can control many aspects of how a worksheet prints directly from the Print screen within Backstage view. For some settings, however, you'll need to use the Page Setup window.

Exam Objective: MOS Excel Core 1.3.4

Printing selected worksheets

Exam Objective: MOS Excel Core 1.5.3

One of the options in the Print screen controls what you will print. There are three choices.

- Click **Print Active Sheets** to print the active worksheet.
- Click **Print Entire Workbook** to print all worksheets in the current workbook.
- Click **Print Selection** to print only the currently selected range.

Controlling scale

 Exam Objective: MOS Excel Core 1.5.4

Use the Print screen's Scaling options to control how much of a worksheet will print on a page.

Scaling Options

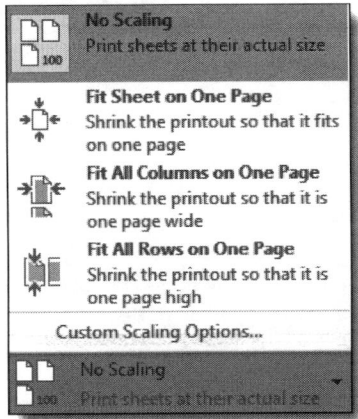

- **No Scaling** prints the worksheet at its current size.
- **Fit Sheet on One Page** does just that. This can be useful, but sometimes results in very small output that is hard to read.
- **Fit All Columns on One Page** is useful when you have a few too many columns to fit on one page. It shrinks the page enough to fit the columns, but not too much to fit a lot of rows.
- **Fit All Rows on One Page** is useful in the opposite situation, when you have a few too many rows to fit.

Controlling orientation

Click **Portrait Orientation** to print a worksheet in a tall format, or **Landscape Orientation** to print it in a wide format. These options are available both in the Print Screen and on the ribbon's Page Layout tab.

 Exam Objective: MOS Excel Core 1.3.4

Printing gridlines or row and column headings

You can specify whether or not to print gridlines or row and column headings on your worksheets.

1. Click the Page Layout tab.
2. In the Sheet Options group, click the options you want:
   - Under Gridlines, click **Print** to show a grid on the printout
   - Under Headings, click **Print** to show row and column headings on the printout.

Controlling margins

Margins are the space around the top, bottom, left, and right edges of your printed worksheets. You can use simple margin settings in the Print screen, or completely custom settings.

Exam Objective: MOS Excel Core 1.3.4

- In the Print screen or on the ribbon's Page Layout tab, select a margin option.

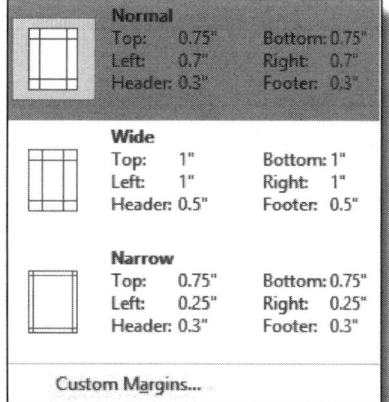

- Click **Custom Margins** to manually set all the margins from the Page Setup window.

Exercise: Controlling print options

Printing Worksheets is open.

Exam Objective: MOS Excel Core 1.3.4, 1.5.3, 1.5.4

Do This	How & Why
1. Activate Reps by Month.	
2. Click **File > Print**.	
3. Click **Print Active Sheets**.	To display the options. Note that you can print the active worksheet, the entire workbook, or just a selection.
4. Press **Esc**.	To close the options for what to print.
5. Observe the preview.	As you've seen, by default, not all of this worksheet fits on a single page.
6. Click the Scaling options, then click **Fit Sheet on One Page**.	The scaling options are at the bottom of the settings. The preview now fits on a single page, but it is awfully small.
7. Click the **Orientation** options, then click **Landscape Orientation**.	A wide presentation looks much better for this worksheet.
8. Press **Esc**.	To return to the worksheet.
9. Specify that you want gridlines.	

Do This	How & Why
a) Click the **Page Layout** tab on the ribbon.	
b) In the Sheet Options group, under Gridlines, check **Print**.	To show gridlines in the printout.
10. Observe the margin options.	
a) Click the **Margins** button.	In the Page Setup group of the Page Layout ribbon tab. Excel gives you simple choices for narrow, wide, or normal margins.
b) Click **Custom Margins**.	To display the Margins tab of the Page Setup window. Here, you can carefully control every margin.
c) Click **Cancel**.	
11. Save the workbook as **My Printing Worksheets**.	

Printing in landscape orientation with gridlines

Sales Rep	Jan	Feb	Mar	Apr	May	Jun	Jul	Aug	Sep	Oct	Nov	Dec	Grand Total
Blackwell	$ 49	$ 405	$ 518	$ 551		$ 502	$ 130	$ 65	$ 437	$ 146	$ 178	$ 65	$ 3,046
Daniels	$ 1,232	$ 1,052	$ 562	$ 689	$ 1,409	$ 993	$ 567	$ 671	$ 833	$ 382	$ 445	$ 373	$ 9,207
Franklin	$ 1,293	$ 715	$ 300	$ 961	$ 1,120	$ 1,190	$ 1,226	$ 963	$ 855	$ 1,241	$ 1,292	$ 1,384	$ 12,539
Hernandez	$ 1,467	$ 1,188	$ 1,847	$ 718	$ 1,734	$ 878	$ 888	$ 1,544	$ 1,092	$ 1,500	$ 2,015	$ 727	$ 15,600
Lloyd	$ 1,840	$ 1,904	$ 1,744	$ 2,737	$ 1,960	$ 1,206	$ 1,829	$ 808	$ 2,141	$ 2,595	$ 2,427	$ 2,201	$ 23,392
McCanney	$ 754	$ 1,046	$ 1,607	$ 2,119	$ 2,255	$ 1,592	$ 3,591	$ 2,974	$ 445	$ 1,165	$ 1,002	$ 1,520	$ 20,067
Patterson	$ 932	$ 389	$ 436	$ 524	$ 517	$ 97	$ 368	$ 273	$ 600	$ 575	$ 728	$ 1,675	$ 7,113
Sanchez	$ 1,254	$ 1,269	$ 950	$ 1,609	$ 728	$ 945	$ 698	$ 2,132	$ 368	$ 731	$ 1,227	$ 995	$ 12,905
Schiller	$ 1,869	$ 1,666	$ 1,365	$ 1,888	$ 893	$ 2,204	$ 1,222	$ 1,374	$ 2,291	$ 1,441	$ 1,278	$ 1,748	$ 19,240
Westlein	$ 842	$ 942	$ 1,959	$ 2,321	$ 1,755	$ 1,254	$ 1,198	$ 859	$ 1,254	$ 2,224	$ 619	$ 1,620	$ 16,846
Grand Total	$ 11,531	$ 10,576	$ 11,287	$ 14,117	$ 12,371	$ 10,861	$ 11,717	$ 11,662	$ 10,317	$ 11,999	$ 11,210	$ 12,307	139,955

Print area and titles

You can set a *print area* to print only the part of a workbook you select. You can also specify print titles, which then appear as headings on every page of your printout.

Setting a print area

 Exam Objective: MOS Excel Core 1.5.1

Set a print area to print only a selected part of a worksheet.

1. Select the range you want to print.
2. On the Page Layout tab, click **Print Area**, then click **Set Print Area**.
3. Print the worksheet.

Only the selected print range prints.

Setting print titles

By setting print titles, you can specify headings that should appear at the top (or on the left) of every page of a printout.

Exam Objective: MOS Excel Core 1.5.5

1. On the Page Layout tab, click **Print Titles**.

    To display the Sheet tab of the Page Setup window. You can get to the Page Setup window in many ways, but several ribbon buttons take you directly to the part of the window where you need to be.

2. Under Print titles, click in the "Rows to repeat at top" box.
3. Click a row heading in the worksheet to enter a reference to the row you want to repeat on each page (usually the column headings for a list).

    If the window is in the way, you can click the collapse button to make the window small.

4. If you want, use the "Columns to repeat at left" box to specify headings to repeat on that side.
5. After specifying the print title row:

    - Click **OK** to accept the titles and return to the worksheet.
    - Click **Print** to send the worksheet directly to the printer.
    - Click **Print Preview** to see a preview of how the printed worksheet will look. This is always a good idea before printing.

Exercise: Setting a print area and printing titles

 Exam Objective: MOS Excel Core 1.5.1, 1.5.5

My Printing Worksheets is open. In this exercise, you'll set a print area to print just the data on a worksheet, and then specify a row to repeat as print titles on all pages.

Do This	How & Why
1. Set a print area on the Invoices worksheet.	
a) Activate the Invoices worksheet.	
b) Select A9:H1007.	Select A9, hold down **Shift** (and keep holding), press **Ctrl+Right Arrow**, then **Ctrl+Down Arrow**. That very quickly selects the range. You can also select A9, scroll to view H1007, and click it while holding down **Shift**.
c) On the Page Layout tab, click **Print Area**, then **Set Print Area**.	
2. Preview the printed worksheet.	Click **File**, then **Print**.
3. Scroll down in the preview.	Notice that the headings appear only on the first page. Also, two columns don't fit on the first page. This would make the printout have far too many pages.
4. Click the **Scaling** button, then click **Fit All Columns on One Page**.	Now all the columns fit. The text is a bit smaller, but it's a better use of space.
5. Return to the worksheet.	Press **Esc**.
6. Repeat row 9 as print titles.	
a) On the Page Layout tab, click **Print Titles**.	The Page Setup window opens with the Sheet tab active.
b) Click in the "Rows to repeat at top" box.	
c) On the worksheet, click the row 9 heading.	A reference to row 9 appears in the box. Print titles Rows to repeat at top: $9:$9 Columns to repeat at left:
7. Click **Print Preview**.	To preview the worksheet.
8. Scroll through the preview.	The headings appear on every page, which makes the data much easier to understand.
9. Close the preview and save the workbook.	

Headers and footers

Headers and *footers* are text, graphics, and codes that you can insert at the top (head) or bottom (foot) of a printed worksheet. You use the Insert tab to create headers and footers by effectively switching to Page Layout view. After you create a header or footer, you can then use buttons to insert information such as page numbers and dates.

Inserting a header or a footer

   Exam Objective: MOS Excel Core 1.3.8

To add a header or footer, start by switching to Page Layout view. When you click in a Header or Footer area, Excel provides a Header & Footer Elements group on a new ribbon tab. You can click those buttons to insert codes that display various kinds of information when you print the worksheet.

The Header & Footer Elements group

Here's how to create a header or a footer:

1. Switch to Page Layout view.

    You can do this by clicking the Page Layout icon on the status bar.

    In Page Layout view you can see how the worksheet will print: headers and footers, page breaks, and print titles. To create headers and footers, simply click in the boxes at the top and bottom of the pages and use the tools on the Header & Footer Tools Design tab.

2. Decide whether you want different odd and even pages or a different first page. Simply click the options you want.

3. Click in the left, center, or right area of the header to activate that position's header box.

4. In the Header box, type any text you want to use as a header. Or, use the Elements buttons to insert codes to show information such as the page number, date, name of the file, name of the sheet, or a picture.

5. On the Home tab, use the formatting tools to format the elements of the header.

6. Click **Go to Footer** to edit the Footer box.

7. Click outside the box to return to the worksheet.

The headers and footers you create appear on the worksheet when you print it, in Page Layout view, and in the Print screen's preview. If you need to adjust the size of the header area, drag the ruler on the left of the header in Page Layout view. To return to the normal view of your worksheet, click **Normal** on the View tab or the Status bar.

Workbook views

 Exam Objective: MOS Excel Core 1.4.5

You can use the workbook views to see how your workbook will look and to more easily control certain aspects of how it will print. Simply click a view icon on the status bar to switch to that view.

1. *Normal* view is the standard Excel view of your workbook. This is the easiest view to work in for creating worksheets, entering formulas and data, and formatting.

2. *Page Layout* view shows what will print and what will not, including any headers and footers on the worksheet.

3. *Page Break Preview* gives you control over the print area, and also over where pages break. This can be very useful when you are trying to get particular data on a particular page.

Exercise: Creating a header and a footer

My Printing Worksheets is open.

 Exam Objective: MOS Excel Core 1.3.8, 1.4.4

Do This	How & Why
1. On the status bar, click [icon].	The Page Layout icon is at the bottom of the screen. Excel switches to Page Layout view, and you now have an editable header area at the top of the worksheet.
2. Insert the sheet name on the left of the header.	
a) Click the left header box.	
b) On the Header & Footer Tools Design tab, click **Sheet Name**.	To insert a code that inserts the sheet name when you print. Header &[Tab]
c) Click the middle header box.	When you move out of the box you're editing, the code becomes the sheet name, "Invoices."
3. Insert the Java Tucana logo in the center of the header.	
a) Click the center header box.	If necessary.
b) Click **Picture**.	The Insert Picture window opens.
c) Next to From a file, click **Browse**.	
Continued...	

Do This	How & Why
d) Navigate to the Output data folder, select **JavaTucanaLogo**, and click **Insert**.	Again, Excel inserts a code.
e) Click the right header box.	So you can see the inserted picture. The header area isn't quite tall enough.
4. Make the header taller.	
a) Point to the bottom of the header ruler.	The pointer changes to a two-headed arrow.
b) Drag down to fit the logo in the header.	
5. In the right header, insert the current date.	
a) Click in the right header.	
b) On the Header & Footer Tools Design tab, click **Current Date**.	The code appears in the box.
c) Click on the worksheet.	To see the date in the header.
6. Make the header text 16 pt, bold.	
a) Select the left header code.	
b) Format it as 16 pt, bold.	On the Home tab, use the formatting tools.
c) Format the right header code.	
7. Preview the printed worksheet.	Scroll through it, and you'll see that the header appears on every page, along with the print titles you set before.
8. Close the preview.	
9. Click in the header, then click the Header & Footer Tools Design tab on the ribbon.	There are options for having a different first page, or different odd and even pages. This can be useful for reports that have headings on the first page, or for printouts that are bound in a book.
10. Click in the worksheet; then click ⊞.	The Normal view icon is on the status bar.
11. Save and then close the workbook.	

Previewing the worksheet with a formatted header

Assessment: Printing worksheets

Where can you find the Print command in Excel?

- On the ribbon's Home tab.
- In Backstage view (by clicking File).
- On the ribbon's Page Layout tab.
- On the ribbon's View tab.

You can control many aspects of how a worksheet prints on the Page Layout tab. True or false?

- True
- False

What is the best way to show column headings on every page of a printout?

- Break your data up and enter headings after every page break.
- On the Page Layout tab, under Headings, click Print.
- Set a row or rows and print titles for the worksheet.

In which view can you create headers and footers?

- Page Layout view
- Page Break preview
- Normal view
- A custom view

The Header & Footer Tools Design tab has tools for formatting. True or false?

- True
- False

Module C: Sharing workbooks

You can share workbooks with other users in an enormous variety of ways: through email, online, and in various formats. You should think about the needs of the person receiving the workbook before you decide on the best way to share it.

You will learn how to:

- Save an Excel workbook in a different format
- Share workbook either as an email attachment, or online by using OneDrive

File formats

Excel 2016 uses the same workbook format as both Excel 2007, Excel 2010, and Excel 2013. You do not need to do anything special to be able to share workbooks with users who have any of those versions of Excel.

But if you are sharing a workbook with a user of a version of Excel before 2007, or someone who does not have Excel, you should save your workbooks to formats that they can use, or that they can at least read. This table lists some useful formats and when you might use them.

Format	Useful when...
Excel 97-2003 Workbook	The people you want to share with use a version of Excel earlier than Excel 2007.
Web page	You want to save a workbook to the web.
CSV	You want to upload the data in a workbook to a web service, such as a mailing list, or you want to read it into a database. There are many varieties of CSV format, which stands for "comma-separated values."
PDF	You don't know much about the people you're sharing with. Anyone can read a PDF document, though, by simply downloading a reader application, but users cannot easily change the data in a PDF.
XPS	You don't know much about the people you're sharing with. Like PDF, XPS is a format anyone can read if they install a free viewer (the viewer is a default part of Windows 7 and higher).
Open Document Spreadsheet	You want to share with users of Open Office, an open-source format for documents and spreadsheets.

Saving to an earlier version of Excel

Exam Objective: MOS Excel Core 1.5.2

If you send an Excel 2016 workbook to a user who has Excel 97, she won't be able to open it. Save to an earlier version of Excel when you want to share a workbook with users of those early versions.

1. In Backstage view, click **Save As**.

    Click File on the ribbon to go to Backstage view.

2. Click a location option or click **Browse**, then navigate to the location in which you want to save, and enter a name for the file.

3. In the "Save as type" list, click the format you want. The two previous formats for Excel files are:

    - Excel 97-2003 Workbook

- Excel 5.0/95 Workbook
- Any other format, including various text formats, web pages, and more

4. Click **Save**.

Depending on what you did in the workbook, you might get a message about the compatibility of some of the workbook's feature's with the previous version of Excel. And it's possible that some features you like won't work for the users with whom you share the workbook.

Saving as PDF or XPS

By saving a workbook as a PDF or XPS file, you can share it with almost any user. *PDF* is an Adobe proprietary format that is based on postscript. Any user who downloads a free reader can read a PDF file on any computer, regardless of operating system. XPS format is similar but is based on XML. It was created originally by Microsoft, but is now an open standard. All newer versions of Windows come with XPS viewers built in, and there are free viewers for other operating systems, including Mac OS.

The problem with this approach is that workbooks saved in this way become snapshots of the workbook, and the users you send them to cannot interact with or change them in any way. That is fine when sending out reports, but not good if you want to collaborate.

1. In Backstage view, click **Export**.

    Excel provides many features for saving workbooks in other formats and sending them to other users.

2. Click **Create PDF/XPS Document**.

    To open the Publish as PDF or XPS window. You can control many aspects of how the workbook is published.

3. Enter a file name.

4. In the "Save as type" list, click the format you want (**PDF** or **XPS Document**).

5. Click to determine whether to open the document and whether to save it at standard or minimum size.

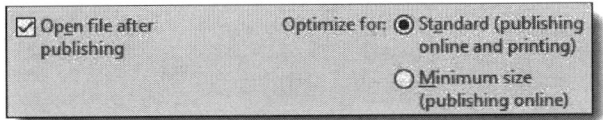

6. Click **Options** to control other options for the saved file.
    - Page range
    - Selection, active sheet, or entire workbook
    - Non-printing information
    - ISO 19005-1 compliance

7. Click **OK** to return to the main window, then click **Publish**.

If you chose to open the published file, it opens in a viewer. This file can now be shared with other users over a network, by email, on a flash drive, or through the Internet.

Exercise: Saving a workbook in other formats

Exam Objective: MOS Excel Core 1.5.2

Do This	How & Why
1. Open Sharing.	From the Output data folder. This workbook contains two report worksheets, and a worksheet of invoice data from which the reports were made.
2. Click **File > Save As**, then click the Output folder.	To open the Save As window. You can save a workbook with a new name, to a new location, or in a different format.
3. Click the "Save as type" box.	To display a list of file types in which you can save the workbook. There are many, all useful in certain circumstances.
4. Observe the Excel 97-2003 option.	Excel changed its file format with the 2007 version. If you are saving a workbook for users with an earlier version than that, you should probably save in this format.
5. Press **Esc**, then click **Cancel**.	To close the window without saving.
6. Click **Export**.	In Backstage view (if it's not showing, click File first). Here, you have options for saving your workbook in various formats.
7. Click **Create PDF/XPS Document**.	The Publish as PDF or XPS window opens, giving you many options for saving your workbook in one of these two formats. The default is to save the workbook as a PDF.
8. Click **Cancel** to close the window.	

Ways to share workbooks

A workbook is just an electronic file, and you can share it with others as you would any other electronic file: by email, on a flash drive, on a work network, or through or on the Internet. A few of the many ways are to send an email attachment, share the workbook on a file-sharing service such as Google Drive or Microsoft's OneDrive, or present the file using an online meeting.

Sending workbooks as email attachments

You can attach a workbook to an email directly from within Excel. Just be sure you have an email program, such as Microsoft Outlook, set up on your computer.

1. In Backstage view, click **Share**.
2. Click **Email**.
   Backstage view displays a list of ways you can send the workbook.
3. Click the way you want to send the workbook.
   - *Send as Attachment* sends the workbook in its current format, attached to an email in your default email program.
   - *Send as Link*, which you can do only if you first save the workbook to a shared location.
   - *Send as PDF* sends the workbook in PDF format, attached to an email in your default email program.
   - *Send as XPS* sends the workbook in XPS format, attached to an email in your default email program.

- *Send as Internet Fax* uses an Internet-based fax service to send a copy of the workbook.
4. In your email program, enter an address and subject line, and then send the email with the attachment.

Sharing workbooks online

There are many ways these days to share a workbook online. If you have a Microsoft or Google account, you can post files to Microsoft's OneDrive or to Google Drive. Then, you can share the location of the workbook or just a link to the file.

Another option is to present your file using an online meeting such as Skype. When you do that, you can give others a guided tour or even, with some services, allow others to control the workbook during the meeting.

Exercise: Sharing a workbook

To perform this task, you need an email client on your computer and a working email account. Your instructor may choose to simply demonstrate this activity. The Sharing workbook should be open at the beginning of the exercise.

Do This	How & Why
1. In Backstage view, click **Share**.	
2. Click **E-mail**, then **Send as Attachment**.	Your email program opens, creates a new message, and attaches the workbook file to it. You can now address the email, add a subject line, and send it.
3. Press **Esc**.	To close the message without sending it.
4. In Backstage view, click **Share**.	You can share a file online after saving it to a shared location such as OneDrive.
5. Click **Present Online**.	You can use this option to start a Skype meeting in which you can present the workbook or allow others to interact with it.
6. Close Sharing.	You do not need to save any changes.

Assessment: Sharing workbooks

Which format is the best option if you want to show a workbook to someone who might not have Excel?

- Excel 97-2003 Workbook
- CSV
- PDF
- Open Document Spreadsheet

You need to open your mail program to send a workbook as an attachment. True or false?

- True
- False

Summary: Output

You should now know how to:

- Split and freeze worksheets, and arrange multiple windows
- Preview and print worksheets; control print setup options, such as scale, orientation, gridlines, and margins; set a print area and print titles that appear on every page; insert and format headers and footers
- Save a workbook to an earlier version of Excel or to portable formats such as PDF and XPS, and share a workbook with another user by attaching it to an email

Synthesis: Output

In this synthesis exercise, you'll split and freeze worksheet panes, change print settings including header and footer information, and output a workbook as a PDF document.

1. Open Output Synthesis. This workbook contains a list of employees, their hire dates, and a calculation of their terms of service.
2. Split the worksheet above row 3.
3. Freeze the column headings in place.
4. Remove the split.
5. Preview the worksheet.
6. Center the workbook horizontally. **Hint**: Use the Margins tab of the Page Setup window.
7. Set row 2 as print titles for the worksheet.
8. Add a header that shows the Java Tucana logo on the left. Make the header taller to accommodate the graphic.
9. Add a center footer that shows the word `Page`, then the page number, then the word `of` surrounded by spaces, then the number of pages. **Hint**: Use the Footer gallery on the left of the Header & Footer Tools Design tab.
10. Preview the worksheet.
11. Return to Normal view.
12. Save the workbook as `My Output Synthesis`.
13. Save the workbook as a PDF document, opening it in a viewer when you do.
14. Exit the Viewer.
15. Close the workbook.

The workbook saved as an XPS document

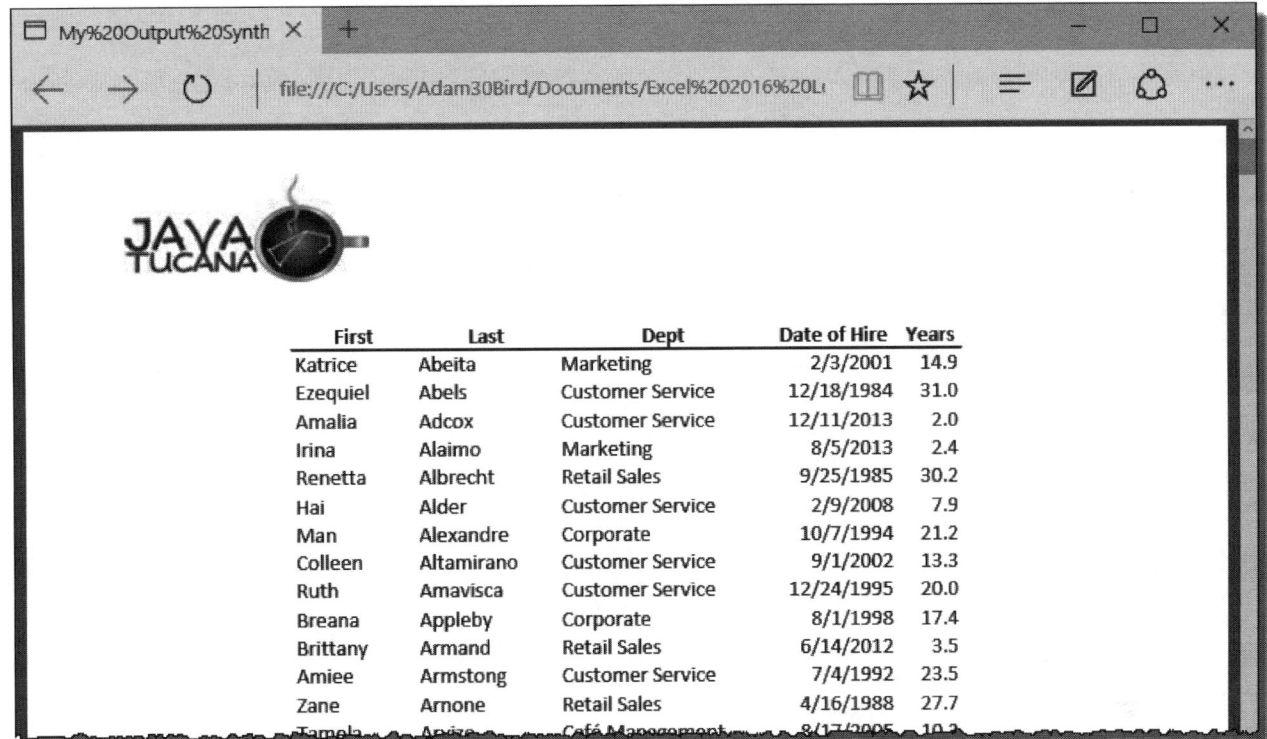

Chapter 7: Settings and templates

You will learn how to:

- Control workbook and worksheet options, as well as workbook properties
- Use templates to create highly functional workbooks quickly

Module A: Workbook options and properties

Excel provides many workbook and worksheet options that control how you interact with Excel, what things look like, and how Excel actually works. You can control an enormous number of these options. Workbooks also have properties that you can change, and these travel with the workbook file, which can be useful when people want to know who created a workbook or what the creator's intent was.

You will learn how to:

- Set options for Excel, for workbooks, and for worksheets
- Set document properties for a workbook
- Inspect a workbook for personal information and compatibility or accessibility issues

Excel options

In Backstage view, you can view and change all sorts of Excel options that control how Excel behaves, when and how files are saved, and how data is presented and processed. Click **Options** in Backstage view, then choose a category. Here are some of the categories, and a few things for which you can use them:

- *General options* give you control over the default font, among other things.
- *Formulas options* control how formulas behave, are calculated, and are checked for errors.
- *Proofing options* provide control over AutoCorrect and checking spelling.
- *Save options* control default file locations and AutoRecover behavior.
- *Language options* give you the ability to add and control the languages used in editing, help, display, and tips.
- *Advanced options* give you control over a huge variety of behaviors for Excel, the current workbook, or the current worksheet.

This is not even close to a complete list; it's just meant to give you an idea of the kinds of things you can do in the Options window.

Changing AutoRecover options

You should save your workbooks often to be sure that you don't lose your work in the event of a software or power problem. But if you don't, Excel has a feature called AutoRecover. By default, Excel occasionally saves your open workbooks, and then if something goes wrong, you can use those automatically saved versions. You can control various aspects of how AutoRecover works by using Excel's Options window.

1. In Backstage view, click **Options**.
2. On the left, click **Save**.
3. Set any options you want.
   - Use the Save AutoRecover information every box to determine how often to save backups of your workbooks.
   - File locations.
   - Exceptions.
4. Click **OK**.

When Excel has saved multiple versions of a workbook, you can use the Manage Versions button on the Info screen in Backstage view to control how those versions are handled.

Managing versions

When Excel automatically saves a version of a workbook, you can then use the Manage Workbook feature to recover any unsaved versions.

 Exam Objective: MOS Excel Expert 1.2.5

1. In Backstage view, click **Info**.

    If there are any autorecovered versions of the file, you will see them listed under Manage Workbooks.

2. Click an autosaved file to open it.
3. Save the autosaved workbook.

    You will get a warning asking if you want to overwrite the current version of the workbook. Be careful that you are saving the version you really want.

Changing advanced options

Excel gives you control over a large range of its behaviors. You can control how Excel takes input, how it calculates, and how specific workbooks and worksheets appear and behave.

 Exam Objective: MOS Excel Core 1.4.8

1. In Backstage view, click **Options**.
2. Click **Advanced**.

    The Advanced options category is enormous.

3. Scroll to find a section you need, and make any changes you want to make. Here are some, but not all, of the useful sections:

    - *Editing options* control over how Excel behaves when you enter data.
    - *Display* controls what parts of the Excel interface and what features appear on screen. These options apply to all of Excel.
    - *Display options for this workbook* and *Display options for this worksheet* apply only to the selected workbook or worksheet, respectively. The worksheet display options include **Show formulas in cells instead of their calculated results**, which can be very useful. You can also toggle the display of formulas in the active worksheet by pressing **Ctrl+`** (grave accent).

4. Click **OK**.

Exercise: Setting Excel options

Exam Objective: MOS Excel Core 1.2.5 and Expert 1.4.8

Do This	How & Why
1. Open Options and Properties.	From the Setting and Templates data folder. This contains monthly sales data by representative.
2. In Backstage view, click **Options**.	Click **File** to get to Backstage view. The Options window gives you control over many things.
3. On the left, click **Save**.	To display the Save options, which include settings for how AutoRecover behaves.
4. In the "Save AutoRecover information every" box, type 15.	To change the interval at which Excel automatically saves workbooks to every 15 minutes. When Excel has automatically saved versions of your workbooks, you can use the Manage Workbook feature on the Info screen in Backstage view to recover changes you may have lost.
5. On the left, click **Formulas**.	Here, you can control how formulas behave and appear, as well as how Excel handles recalculation.
6. On the left, click **Advanced**.	To display the advanced options. There are many categories, and many options.
7. Observe the Editing options section.	You can control what happens when you press Enter, whether fill handles appear on selected cells, and much more.
8. Scroll to observe the Display section.	Here, you can control how many recent workbooks you see, whether to display the formula bar, and whether you see function ScreenTips. These settings apply to all of Excel.
9. Scroll to observe the "Display options for this workbook" section.	For a specific workbook, you can control the display of scroll bars and sheet tabs, and other options.
10. Scroll to observe the "Display options for this worksheet" section.	For the specific worksheet, you have control over the display of formulas, gridlines, row and column headings, zero values, and more. Displaying formulas can be very useful when you are trying to troubleshoot your workbooks. You can toggle the display of formulas by pressing **Ctrl+`** (grave accent)
11. Click **OK**.	To close the Options window and accept any changes.

Workbook properties

Document properties, such as the author, title, and keywords, travel with the file. This is useful, because these properties can be seen in an Explorer window without actually opening a workbook. You can use document properties to let other users know who created a workbook and what kind of information it contains. They're also helpful for reminding yourself why you created a workbook.

Setting document properties

 Exam Objective: MOS Excel Core 1.4.6

1. In Backstage view, click **Info**.
   To display information about the current workbook. There is a list of properties on the right.
2. To change a property, click its associated box and type. Here are some of the properties:
   - *Author* can be your name, or the person who originally created the workbook.
   - *Title* is for the workbook as a whole, and can be different from the file name (although that might be confusing).
   - *Subject* can describe the subject matter of the workbook.
   - *Keywords* can help in finding the workbook in searches.
   - *Comments* are comments that travel with the workbook. If you're sharing the workbook with a coworker, you can pass information to her this way.
3. To view and change more properties, click **Show All Properties**.

The document properties travel with the workbook, and you can see them either here in Backstage view, or by pointing to the workbook in an Explorer window. If you do that, you see the properties in a ScreenTip box.

Exercise: Setting properties for a workbook

Exam Objective: MOS Excel Core 1.4.6

The Options and Properties workbook should be open.

Do This	How & Why
1. In Backstage view, click **Info**.	Notice that there is a list of properties on the right side of the Info screen.
2. Click next to "Author," then type your name.	Click where it says "Add and author."
3. Click **Show All Properties**.	To show all the available properties on the Info screen.
4. In the Subject box, type `Sales report by month and representative`.	
5. In the Comments box, type `Need to check these figures with the Sales Manager`.	
6. Save the workbook as `My Options and Properties`, then close it.	
7. Open a File Explorer window, and navigate to the `Settings and Templates` data folder.	Follow your instructor's directions.
8. Point to the My Options and Properties file.	A ScreenTip appears showing the properties you set for the workbook.
9. Close the File Explorer window.	

Inspecting workbooks

Excel's Inspect Workbooks feature allows you to find, and then in some cases, correct or remove, issues that might exist in your workbooks.

- Hidden properties
- Personal information
- Accessibility issues
- Compatibility issues

1. Click **File > Info**.

    The Info screen gives you control over the workbooks options and properties.

2. Click Next to Inspect Workbook, click **Check for Issues**.

    To display the Inspect Workbook gallery. You can inspect different parts of the workbook for various kinds of issues.

    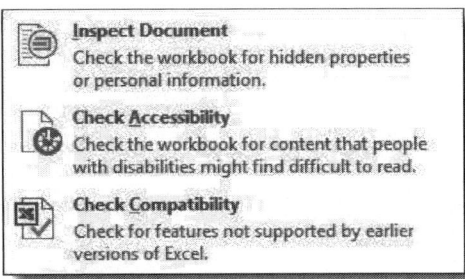

3. Click the option you want, then continue to follow the steps for the particular inspection procedure.

Removing hidden properties and personal information

Some information about a workbook travels with its properties. This can include properties you've set intentionally, and some you have not. Before you distribute a workbook, you might want to remove personal information, such as your name, from the workbook file.

 Exam Objective: MOS Excel Core 1.5.6

1. On the Info screen in Backstage view, click **Inspect Workbook > Inspect Document**.

    To display the Document Inspector window. You can inspect various parts of the workbook for various kinds of information.

    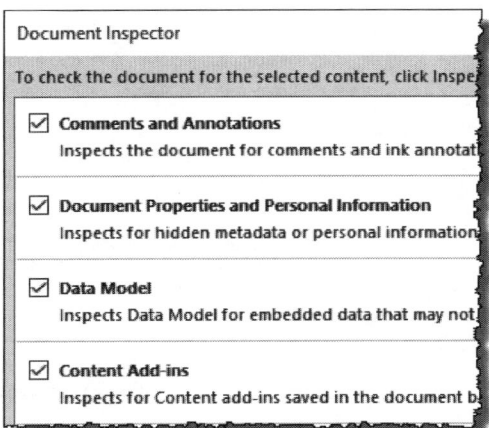

2. Check the options you want, then click **Inspect**.

    To display the inspection results.

3. Next to the Document Properties and Personal Information, click **Remove All**.

4. Close the Document Inspector.

Checking accessibility

The accessibility checker can help you to find and remove issues that users with special needs might have with your workbooks.

 Exam Objective: MOS Excel Core 1.5.7

1. Click **Check for Issues > Check Accessibility**.
   On the Info screen of Backstage view.

   You return to the workbook, but with the Accessibility Checker open on the right side of the screen.

2. Select an issue.
   In the Accessibility Checker.

   It shows you a description of why the issue matter, and a explanation of how to fix the issue.

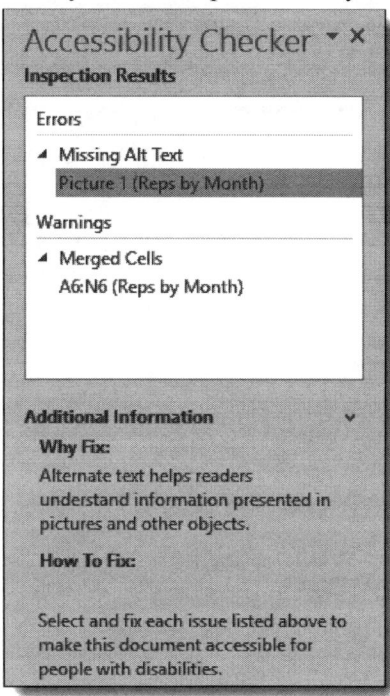

3. Fix any issues.
   As you fix issues, they will disappear from the Accessibility Checker. You do not need to run it again.

4. Close the Accessibility Checker.

Checking compatibility

The Compatibility Checker helps you to find issues that might exist if you send your workbook to users of earlier versions of Excel. If the issues found are important, you should consider modifying your workbook to avoid them.

 Exam Objective: MOS Excel Core 1.5.8

1. Click **Check for Issues > Check Compatibility**.

    On the Info screen in Backstage view.

    To display the Compatibility Checker. If it finds anything about your workbook that might not work with previous versions of Excel, it will list those issues.

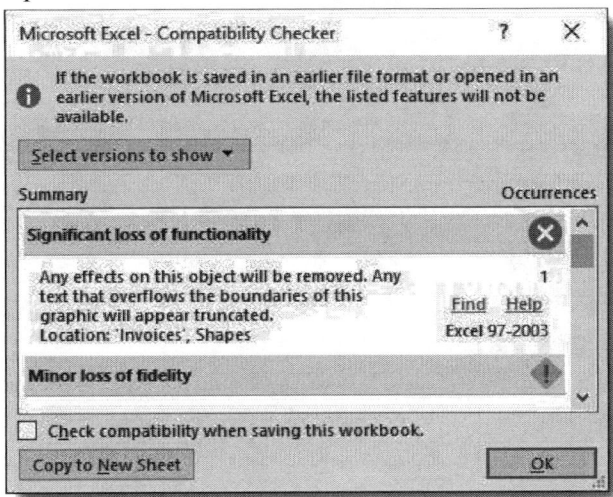

2. If you want to check compatibility only with particular versions of Excel, select the ones you want in the "Select versions to show list."
3. Read through the found issues, then click **OK**.

    To return to the workbook.
4. Make any changes you want to for the sake of compatibility, then run the Compatibility Checker again.

Exercise: Removing personal information and checking accessibility

Exam Objective: MOS Excel Core 1.5.6, 1.5.7

Do This	How & Why
1. Open **My Options and Properties**.	From the `Setting and Templates` data folder. You will inspect this workbook to find any personal information, then remove it. You'll also check the workbook for accessibility issues.
2. Click **File > Info**.	Notice the name of the author and other properties on the right.
3. Click **Check for Issues > Inspect Document**.	If you get a message warning you to save your workbook before inspecting it, click **Yes**. The Document Inspector window appears, giving you options for what you want to inspect.
4. Click **Inspect**.	To inspect the workbook. The Inspector found some personal information. Review the inspection results. ✓ **Comments and Annotations** No items were found. ! **Document Properties and Personal Information** The following document information was found: * Document properties * Author * Related people * Absolute path to the workbook
5. Click **Remove All**.	To remove the personal information.
6. Click **Close**.	You should still be in Backstage view. The name of the author and other personal information about the file are gone.
7. Click **Check for Issues > Check Accessibility**.	On the Info screen in Backtage view. This returns you to the workbook and opens the Accessibility Checker on the right.
8. Click **Picture 1 (Reps by Month)**.	In the Accessibility Checker. To display information about the issue and how to fix it.
9. Add alternate text for the Java Tucana logo.	
a) Right click the log, then click **Format Picture**.	To display the properties window for the image.

Do This	How & Why
b) Display the Alt Text properties.	Click the Size & Properties icon, then expand the Alt Text category.
c) In the Title box, type `Java Tucana logo`.	
d) Close the Properties pane.	
10. Observe the Accessibility Checker.	The alt text issue is no longer shown because you've fixed it.
11. Discuss the other issue, then close the Accessibility Checker.	Discuss some of the tradeoffs in fixing some accessibility issues.
12. Save and close the workbook.	

Assessment: Workbook options and properties

You can control display options for Excel as a whole, for a particular workbook, or for a particular worksheet. True or false?

- True
- False

The document property called "Title" is the same as the workbook's file name. True or false?

- True
- False

What is the best way to remove personal information from a workbook's properties? Choose the best answer.

- Remove the properties carefully, one at a time.
- Use the Document Inspector.
- Copy all of its data to a new, blank workbook.

After attempting to fix an accessibility issue, you must choose the Check Accessibility command again to see if you've fixed the issue. True or false?

- True
- False

Module B: Templates

Templates provide a quick way to get a head start on creating workbooks. A template already has structure, formatting, headings, and formulas created for a particular purpose, like an invoice or a sales report, so you can just start entering data. You can work with built-in templates, download templates from Microsoft, or create your own.

You will learn how to:

- Create a workbook based upon a template
- Save a workbook as a template

Using templates

You often create the same sort of workbooks over and over: schedules, reports, invoices, and so on. *Templates* are a special type of Excel workbook that you can use as a starting point for other workbooks. Excel comes with some templates built in as samples, and you can access a huge variety online. You can also create your own templates.

When you create a workbook from a template, you don't actually open the template file, but rather create a copy of it. That way, the template can be used over and over, without your having to worry about accidentally making changes to it.

Creating workbooks based on templates

All workbooks are actually based upon a template. The standard, blank workbook is a template with nothing in it. You can base workbooks on a wide variety of templates that you can get from various sources.

Exam Objective: MOS Excel Core 1.1.1

1. In Backstage view, click **New**.
    Excel gives you a wide choice of templates to use, plus the ability to search for one.

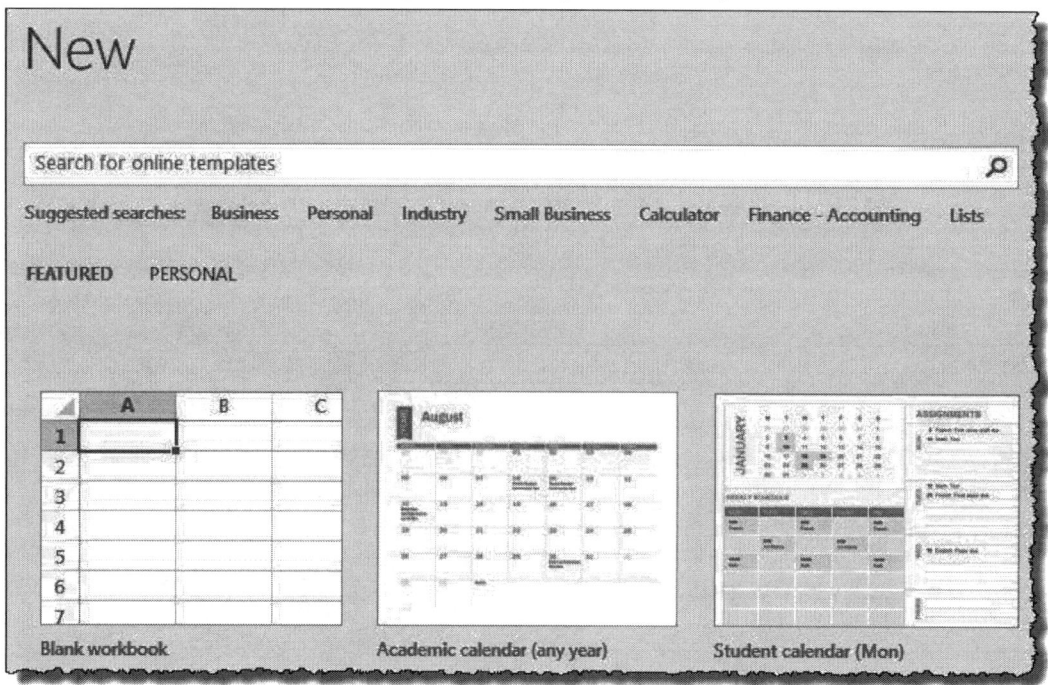

2. You can select one of the templates that is shown, or search for one, either by typing in the search box or by clicking one of the suggested searches.

3. Click a template you want to see a preview. If you like what you see, click **Create**.
   The exception is the Blank workbook template; clicking that leads immediate to opening a new, blank workbook.

Excel creates a new workbook based upon the template. It has data, structure, formulas, formatting, and even programmed automation to help you accomplish a goal. Don't forget to save the workbook when you've entered some of your own information.

Exercise: Experimenting with templates

You will need to have online access to get the Microsoft Expense Report template used in this activity. If you do not have access, your instructor can show you a different template.

Exam Objective: MOS Excel Core 1.1.2

Do This	How & Why
1. In Backstage view, click **New**.	Excel displays tiles associated with various templates, as well as a search box that you can use to search through thousands of online templates.
2. Click one of the template tiles other than Blank Workbook.	You see a preview of the template, and a Create button that you can use to create a new workbook based upon this template.
3. Close the preview of the template.	Click its Close button.
4. In the Search box, type `expense report`, then press **Enter**.	Excel displays a list of available expense report templates.
5. Click the first Expense Report template, then click **Create**.	Excel downloads the template, then a new workbook appears called "Expense report1." This workbook almost doesn't look like Excel, but it is. It has formatting and functionality that would take time and expertise to set up.
6. Enter the following information: a) Under the Date column, in row 11, enter today's date. b) Under Description, type `Lunch`. c) Under Meals, type `12.50`.	
7. Select L11.	This is the last cell in the row, under "Total." Note that the total was calculated for you.
8. Press **Tab**.	You move to the beginning of the next row.
9. Save the workbook as `My Expense report1`.	Save it in the `Settings and Templates` data folder.

Excel 2016 Level 1

An expense report based on the sample template

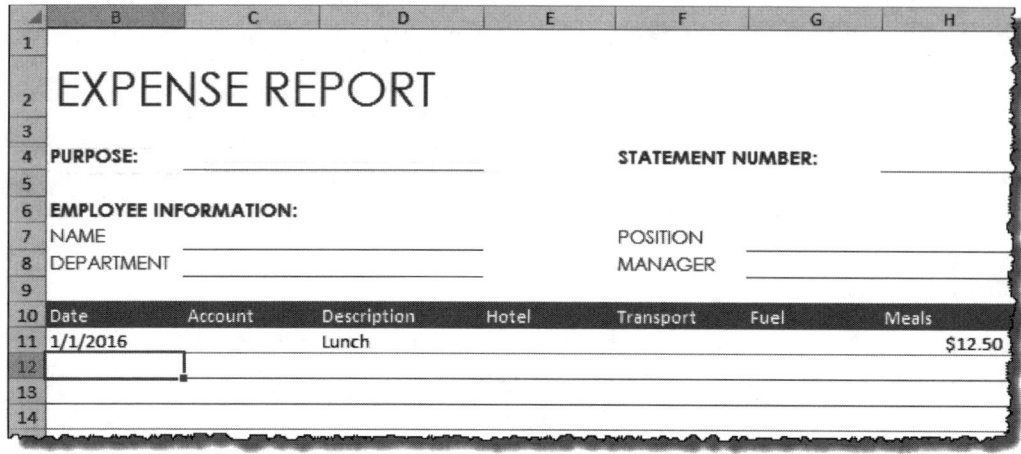

Creating templates

Exam Objective: MOS Excel Expert 1.1.1

To create a template that you can reuse later:

1. Create a workbook that contains all of the design, labels, functionality, and formatting you want.
   Do not include specific data, though. The only elements that should be in a template are the ones you want every time you create a workbook based upon the template.
2. In Backstage view, click **Save As**, then click **Browse**.
   To open the Save As window.
3. In the Save as type box, click **Excel Template**.
   When you specify that you want to save a workbook as a template, Excel automatically moves you to the default template folder for your installation of Excel. You can save a template somewhere else, but then you might have a hard time finding it. By saving it in the default folder, the template appears in the Personal category when you create new workbooks. You can change your default templates folder by using the Save area in the Excel Options window.
4. Type a file name for the template, and then click **Save**.
5. Close the template file.
   This is actually important. Once you save the workbook as a template, it's best not to change it anymore.

You can now create new workbooks based on the template, the way you would using any template. It appears in a Personal category on the New screen in Backstage view.

Editing a template

If you want to edit a template, rather than just create a workbook based on it, the hard part is sometimes finding the Templates folder. The default path is `Documents\Custom Office Templates`, but it can be other places.

1. In Backstage view, click **Open**.
2. Navigate to the Custom Office Templates folder.
3. Select the template you want to edit, then click **Open**.

4. Edit the template as you wish, save it, then close it.

   When you open a template in this way, Excel knows to save it as a template-type file.

Exercise: Creating your own expense report template

Exam Objective: MOS Excel Expert 1.1.1

My Expense report1 is open.

Do This	How & Why
1. Observe My Expense Report.	It will be more useful to you in the future if it already has your name filled in. You'll make that change, then save this workbook as a new template that you can use in the future.
2. Delete the expense data you entered in the workbook.	The date, the description, and the meal amount. You do not want specific data in a template. You want only information that does not change with every use.
3. Under Employee Information, enter your name.	
4. In Backstage view, click **Save As**, then click **Browse**.	
5. In the "Save as type" list, click **Excel Template**.	Notice that the folder changes to the Custom Office Templates folder. By saving templates here, you can always access them easily when creating new workbooks.
6. Ensure that the file name is still My Expense report1.	
7. Click **Save**.	
8. Close My Expense report1.	
9. Create a new workbook based on your template.	
a) In Backstage View, click **New**.	
b) Click **Personal**.	Next to Featured, not in the suggested searches. To view your custom, personal templates.
c) Click **My Expense report1**.	The new workbook includes your name.
10. Close the workbook without saving it.	

Assessment: Templates

When you create a new workbook from a template, you are editing the actual template. True or false?

- True
- False

Which of the following are reasons to save a template in the default templates folder? Choose all that apply.

- Because you cannot save them anywhere else.
- Because the template shows up with your others in the Personal category when you create new files.
- Because it is easy to find when you want to edit it.

Data is not stored with a template. True or false?

- True
- False

Summary: Settings and templates

You should now know how to:

- Control options for Excel, for workbooks, and for worksheets, including display options and AutoRecover behavior; set properties panel for a workbook; use Document Inspector to remove personal information from a workbook; check workbooks for accessibility and compatibility issues
- Use templates to create highly functional workbooks quickly, and turn your own workbooks into templates on which to base future workbooks

Synthesis: Settings and templates

In this synthesis exercise, you'll open a customer information workbook, check it for accessibility issues, adjust some of its display options and properties, then save it as a template.

1. Open Customer Info Form from the Settings and Templates data folder.
   This is a simple form for entering customer information.
2. Check the workbook for accessibility issues, and correct any you find based on the information in the Compatibility Checker.
3. Change the display options for the worksheet to not show gridlines.
4. Add a Comment property about this being a draft for the new customer acquisition process.
5. Save the workbook as a template called `My Customer Info Form`, in the Custom Office Templates folder.
6. Close the template.
7. Create a new workbook based upon the template.
8. Close the workbook without saving it, then exit Excel.

A customer form workbook based on the template

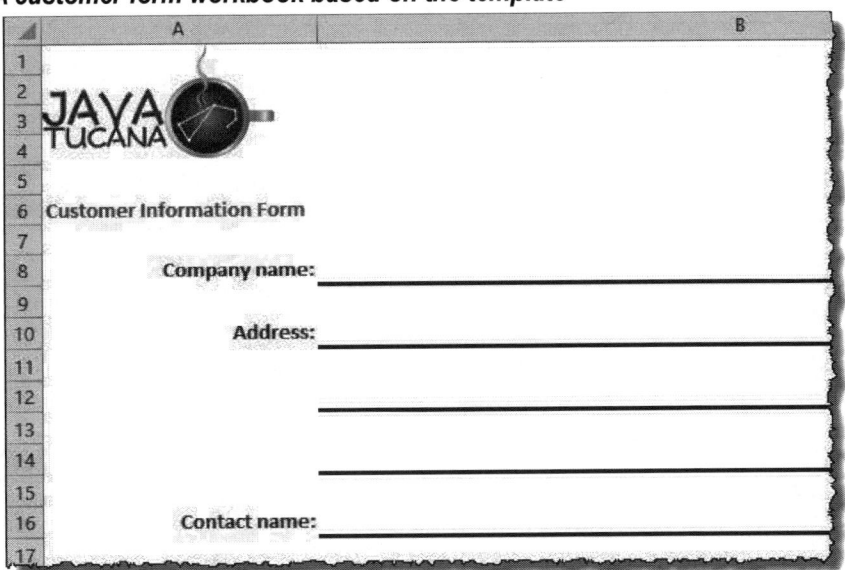

Alphabetical Index

Absolute references 53
    About 53
    Inserting in formulas 53
Accessibility 158, 160
    Checking 160
Alignment 69
    About 69
    Buttons 69
    Controlling 69
Arguments 35
Auto fill 90
    About 90
AutoRecover options 154
AutoSum 40
Borders 75
    About 75
    Applying 75
    Drawing 75
Cell references 28
    Entering in formulas 28
    Using the mouse to enter 28
Cell styles 79, 80
    Applying 79
    Creating 80
Cells 5, 104
    Deleting 104
    Inserting 104
Chart types 117, 118
    Changing 118
    Column 117
    Line 117
Charts 112, 113, 114, 120, 121, 122
    About 112
    Controlling elements 122
    Creating 113
    Elements of 121
    Source data 114
    Switching rows and columns 120
Closing workbooks 16
Column headings 5
Column width 23
    Changing 23
Columns 23, 104, 107
    Changing width 23
    Deleting 104
    Hiding and unhiding 107
    Inserting 104
Compatibility 158, 161
    Checking 161
Copy button 46
Copying data 46
    By dragging 46
    By using Copy and Paste 46
Cut command 43
Data 14, 22
    Entering 14
    Types 22
Dates 66

    Formats 66
    Serial number storage 66
Deleting 104
    Rows and columns 104
Deleting data 23
Document properties 157
    About 157
    Setting 157
Edit mode 32
Email attachments 148
Enter box 14
Entering data 14, 26
    In a range 26
Excel 4
    Starting 4
Fill commands 90
    About 90
    Using 90
Find 12
Find and replace 94
Font group 60
Formats 80, 100
    Clearing 80
    Pasting 100
Formatting 60, 63, 76
    Fill color 76
    Highlighting 76
    Numbers 63
    Text 60
Formula bar 5
Formulas 28, 32, 47, 100
    About 28
    Copying 47
    Elements of 28
    Entering 28
    Pasting 100
    Revising 32
Freezing panes 129
Functions 35, 38
    About 35
    Arguments 35
    Inserting 38
    Structure of 35
Go To 12
Headers and footers 142
    About 142
    Inserting 142
Highlighting 76
Inserting 104
    Rows and columns 104
Inspect Workbook 158
    Accessibility 158
    Compatibility 158
Keyboard 9
    Navigation shortcuts 9
Line charts 112
    About 112
Links 102

Alphabetical Index

About...102
    Pasting..102
Margins..138
Merging cells..72
    About..72
Mixed references..55
    About..55
    Inserting in formulas................................55
Moving data..43, 44
    By dragging..44
    By using Cut and Paste............................43
Navigation..12
    Go To..12
    Searching..12
Non-contiguous ranges......................................61
Number formats..63, 64
    About..63
    Applying..64
    Categories..63
Numbers..22, 26
    About..22
    Display of..26
    Entering..26
Opening workbooks..8
Options..154, 155
    About..154
    Advanced..155
Order of operations..31
Orientation..137
Page Break preview..143
Page Layout view......................................142, 143
Page setup..136
    About..136
Paste button..46
Paste command..43
Paste options..100
    About..100
    Button..100
PDF format..147
Personal information..159
    Removing..159
Pie charts..112
    About..112
Previewing..135
Print area..140
Print titles..140
Printing............................135, 136, 137, 138, 140, 142
    About..135
    Gridlines..137
    Headers and footers..............................142
    Margins..138
    Orientation..137
    Previewing..135
    Print area..140
    Print titles..140
    Requirements for....................................135
    Row and column headings....................137
    Scale..137
    Selected worksheets..............................136

    Worksheets..135
Quick Access toolbar..5
R1C1 reference style..50
Ranges..9, 26, 64, 104
    About..9
    Deleting..104
    Entering data in..26
    Inserting..104
    Selecting with the keyboard....................64
Redo button..44
References types..50
    About..50
    Absolute..50
    Relative..50
Relative references..51
    Limitations of..51
Replacing data..94
Ribbon..5
Row headings..5
Rows..104, 107
    Deleting..104
    Hiding and unhiding..............................107
    Inserting..104
Save As command..15
Saving workbooks..15
Scale..137
Scientific notation..26
Selecting..61
    Multiple ranges..61
Selecting ranges..64
    Using the keyboard..................................64
Sharing..148
    About..148
Splitting windows..128
Starting Excel..4
Styles..80
    Tables..80
SUM()..40
    Entering using AutoSum..........................40
Tables..80
    Styles..80
Templates..164, 166
    About..164
    Create workbooks based on..................164
    Creating..166
    Editing..166
Text..22, 23
    About..22
    Alignment of..23
    Entering..23
Text formatting..60
Themes..84
Undo button..44
Value axis..122
    Controlling..122
Values..100
    Pasting..100
Vertical alignment..70
    Setting..70

Windows 128, 129, 131, 132
    Arranging 128, 131, 132
    Freezing panes 129
    Opening new 132
    Splitting 128
Workbook views 143
    About 143
Workbooks 8, 9, 15, 16, 24, 146, 147, 148, 149, 155, 157, 158
    Attaching to email 148
    Closing 16
    Creating new 24
    Inspecting 158
    Managing versions 155
    Navigating 9
    Opening 8
    Properties 157

    Recovering unsaved 155
    Saving 15
    Saving in other formats 146
    Saving to earlier versions 146
    Saving to PDF 147
    Saving to XPS 147
    Sharing 148
    Sharing online 149
    Zooming 9
Worksheet 5
Worksheet tabs 9
Worksheets 29, 128
    Design considerations 29
    Splitting 128
Wrapping text 70
XPS format 147